W9-AXX-211

The HISTORY *of* ART

From Ancient to Modern Times

Claudio Merlo

ILLUSTRATED BY
Manuela Cappon, L. R. Galante, Giacinto Gaudenzi,
Andrea Ricciardi, Claudia Saraceni, Sergio, Francesco Spadoni

PETER BEDRICK BOOKS
NTC/Contemporary Publishing Group

DoGi

Produced by:
DoGi spa, Florence, Italy
Original title:
Atlante dell'arte
Text:
Claudio Merlo
Illustrations:
Alessandro Bartolozzi, Simone Boni, Manuela Cappon, Lorenzo Cecchi, L. R. Galante, Giacinto Gaudenzi, Alessandro Menchi, Tiziano Perotto, Sandro Rabatti, Andrea Ricciardi, Claudia Saraceni, Sergio, Alessandro Spadoni, Ivan Stalio, Studio Inklink, Thomas Troyer
Design:
Laura Ottina
Editing:
Leonardo Cappellini, Francesco Milo
Art Director:
Sebastiano Ranchetti
English translation:
Nathaniel Harris
Editing, English-language edition:
Ruth Nason

Library of Congress Cataloging-in-Publication data is available from the United States Library of Congress

First published in the United States in 2000 by PETER BEDRICK BOOKS
A division of NTC/Contemporary Publishing, Group Inc.
4255 West Touhy Avenue, Lincolnwood (Chicago),
Illinois 60712-1975 U.S.A.

Printed in Italy
ISBN: 0-87226-531-5

99 00 01 02 03   16 15 14 13 12 11 10 9 8 7 6 5 4 3 2 1

Credits

Abbreviations: *b*, bottom; *c*, center; *l*, left; *r*, right; *t*, top.

ILLUSTRATIONS
The illustrations in this book may only be reproduced with the prior permission of DoGi spa, who hold the copyright.
Inside: Archivio DoGi: 54-55; Giovanni Bernardi: 9br; Simone Boni: 78–79, 118–19; Simone Boni and Lorenzo Cecchi: 62c; Simone Boni and L. R. Galante: 106l; Lorenzo Cecchi: 42–43; Luciano Crovato and Gianni Mazzoleni: 62b, 96t, 102–3; Giacinto Gaudenzi: 16–17, 18–19, 24–25, 43b, 92–93; Paola Holguin: 89b; Tiziano Perotto: 44–45; Sandro Rabatti: 53tr, 58–59; Andrea Ricciardi: 49a, 76–77, 84–85, 86–87, 88–89; Sergio: 10–11, 12, 26–27, 46–47, 48–49, 50–51, 64–65, 70–71, 82–83, 114–15, 124; Claudia Saraceni: 90–91, 94–95, 116–117, 120–121; Studio Boni-Pieri-Critone: 53bt, 104–5; Studio Galante: L. R. Galante: 36–37, 63c, 66–67, 68–69, 72–73, 74–75, 98–99, 108–9, 110–11, 122–23, L. R. Galante and Manuela Cappon: 34–35, Manuela Cappon: 32–33, 60–61, Alessandro Menchi: 100–1, Francesco Spadoni: 12–13, 28–29, 40–41, 56–57, 97b, Ivan Stalio: 40–41, 112–13; Studio Inklink: 14–15, 20–21; Thomas Troyer: 30–31
Maps: Alessandro Bartolozzi
Cover illustrations: Andrea Ricciardi tr; Sergio br
Back cover illustration: L. R. Galante

PHOTOGRAPHS AND DOCUMENTS
DoGi spa has made every effort to trace other possible copyright holders. If any omissions or errors have been made, they will be corrected at reprint.
Inside: Alinari, Florence: 77, 82, 92; Alinari/Giraudon, Florence, Paris: 9cr, 9bl, 16, 18, 22b, 63cr, 67, 81b, 119; Artephot/M. Babey, Paris: 107tl; Artothek, Munich: 107tr; Bildkunstverlag Gerhard/Waltraud Klammer, Germering: 39br; Sergio Bottai: 8tl; Bridgeman Art Library, London: 23tl, 68, 96c, 106b, 107bl, 120; Curcio: 39b; DoGi, Florence: 8cl, 9tr, 12, 14, 20, 22t, 24, 26, 31, 32, 34, 37, 39tl, 39tr, 39t, 40, 52t, 52c, 52b, 53c, 54, 57, 59, 60, 62c, 62b, 63br, 63tr, 80b, 81br, 87, 91, 97l, 99, 104, 106t, 107c, 122; DoGi, Florence/Mario Quattrone: 49b, 51, 64, 89b; DoGi, Florence/Serge Domingie-Marco Rabatti: 63bc, 63bl; Electa: 94; Fotostock, Barcelona: 9tl; Franco Cosimo Panini, Modena: 46t, 46b; Giunti: 80t; Igda, Novara: 16; Erich Lessing, Vienna: 62t, 81cr, 89t; Metropolitan Museum, New York: 96b, 110t; Museo Pigorini, Rome: 53bl, 97c, 103; Museum für Völkerkunde, Berlin: 100; Museum Ludwig/Rheinisches Bildarchiv, Cologne: 107br; Naturhistorisches Museum, Vienna: 10; Private collection: 97t; Rijksmuseum Vincent Van Gogh: 112; Rizzoli, Milan: 81t; Sarnath Archeological Museum: 28; Scala, Florence: 8b, 44, 70, 80c, 97t, 109; Statens Konstmuseum, Stockholm: 107cr, 110b; Staatliche Museen, Berlin: 23br; Staatsgalerie, Stuttgart: 114; Thames and Hudson, Berlin: 23tr, 23c; Tretyakov Gallery, Moscow: 117; Uffizi Gallery, Florence: 78; Vatican Museums, Rome: 72, 74; Peter Willi, Paris: 23, 43t, 80, 84.
Cover: Alinari/Giraudon, Florence, Paris: bl; DoGi: tl, tr; DoGi/Mario Quattrone: tc, cl.

Contents

Art That Defies Time

The East

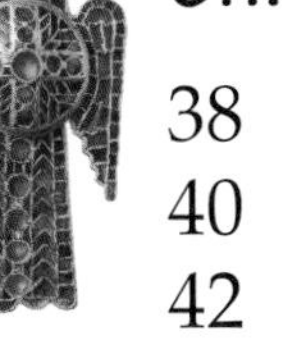

Christian Art

The New World

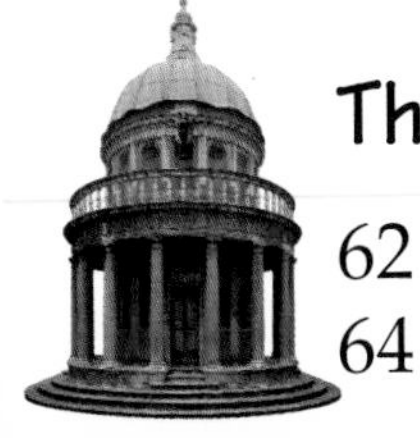

The Renaissance

The Rise of Europe

Africa and the Pacific

Break with Tradition

Art That Defies Time

This first chapter does not try to pinpoint the origin of art to a single place. It describes the most ancient works of which traces survive, from western Europe, the Mediterranean, and the continents of Asia and Africa. These works were created late in the prehistoric period and during the earliest phases of recorded history. They have been able to defy the passing of time, thanks to the durable nature of the materials used by some ancient peoples, the vagaries of history, and, not least, the wonderful discoveries made over the centuries by archeologists and explorers.

Standing stones at Palaggiu, Corsica

Our journey

The human species developed very slowly, over millions of years, from pre-human primate ancestors. Twenty thousand years ago, in the Upper Paleolithic period (the most recent phase of the Old Stone Age), European hunter-gatherers painted pictures which are still visible today on the walls of caves at Lascaux, France (pages 10–11). Then, at the end of the last Ice Age, population increased, and in this, the Neolithic period, the first agricultural communities developed. These in turn gave rise to the first cities and states, and art became an expression of religious devotion and political power. There were great collective undertakings: for example, the pyramids of ancient Egypt (pages 12–13) are still awe-inspiring, and the same is true of Stonehenge, the stone circle created by a prehistoric people in Great Britain (pages 14–15). Later, in the Mediterranean, the art of classical Greece emerged. Greek architects built temples of unparalleled beauty (pages 16–17) and Greek sculptors excelled in carving and bronze-casting (pages 18–19). Finally, Rome conquered the entire area we have described, and Roman builders exploited the technique of using the arch (pages 20–21) to accomplish ever-greater feats of architecture and engineering.

Neolithic Europe
From the beginning of the 5th millennium B.C., huge stone monuments were erected in northern Europe, especially in the British Isles, western France, and the Iberian peninsula.

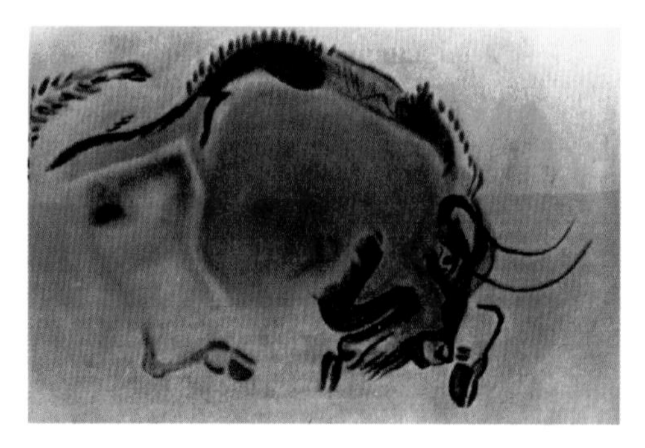

Bison, the cave at Altamira, Spain

Paleolithic Europe
Prehistoric cave paintings are concentrated in the Dordogne area of France and in the Iberian peninsula. But there are many other sites with mural (wall) art, for example in Italy, Portugal, Romania, and Russia.

Rome
Once a small city-state, Rome became the largest empire in the ancient world by the 1st century A.D. Its territory stretched from Spain to central Europe, from North Africa to Mesopotamia

Trajan's Column, Rome

Theater at Epidaurus, Greece

Greece
Developing during the 1st millennium B.C., Greek civilization was based on the polis, or independent city-state. The most famous of the many city-states was 5th-century Athens.

Lion, glazed brick, from the processional way in Babylon

Babylon
Under King Nebuchadrezzar, in the 6th century B.C., Mesopotamia again became powerful. In Babylon, temples, hanging gardens, and perhaps the mythical Tower of Babel, were built.

Assyrian winged guardian

Nineveh
Early in the 1st millennium, the Assyrians created an empire which took in all of Mesopotamia. In the capital, Nineveh, bas-reliefs illustrated the empire's military might.

Egypt
Having unified Egypt at the end of the 4th millennium B.C., the Egyptian kings had the pyramids built as tombs for themselves during the Old Kingdom period (3rd millennium B.C.).

Head of the Egyptian queen Nefertiti

Ur
Mesopotamia was a cradle of great cultures. In the first of these, the Sumerian civilization (3rd millennium B.C.), the temple was the center of the city of Ur.

Ziggurat

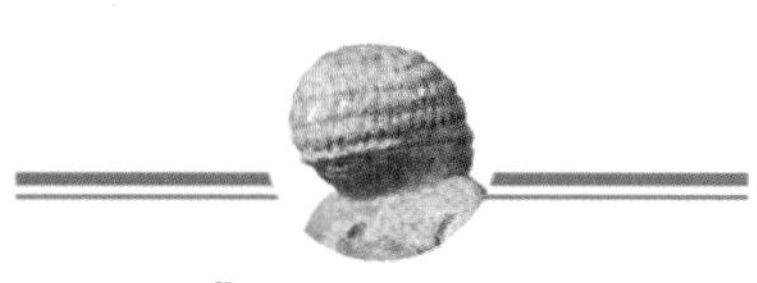

Cave art

The hunters of the European Upper Paleolithic, which began in about 35,000 B.C., made many wall paintings as well as carvings in stone, ivory, and bone. The famous paintings in the cave of Lascaux, France, date from about 15,000 B.C.

Representation
The hunters were probably less interested in the final look of the picture than in the magical act of representing an animal, which was intended to ensure a successful hunt.

The Venus of Willendorf

Sculpture in limestone, 4½ in. high, 20,000 B.C., Natural History Museum, Vienna

This and other "Venus" carvings were fertility figures, not just representations or symbols of femininity. Such figures date from the Upper Paleolithic period, during which significant developments were made in the art of carving. The association of the image of a woman with fertility probably came to be used to guarantee the survival of the group. These figures have very pronounced breasts, buttocks, and hips, and the detailed rendering of the hair is achieved by a characteristic pattern.

Arrow marks
Arrow marks, often found on or near the figures of the animals, were probably made by hunters as part of some magical rite – imitating a killing to make it happen.

The animals
There are pictures of horses, wild oxen, deer, ibex, reindeer, and a unicorn-like beast. A line of five stags' heads has been interpreted as showing a single animal at different moments, swimming across a stretch of water.

The discovery at Lascaux
The paintings were found by two boys in 1940. The cave is less than 330 feet long. Almost as soon as you enter, you see an amazing assembly of large animals.

The tomb of Tuthmosis

Wall painting, detail, c. 1450 B.C., Valley of the Kings, Egypt

In Egypt, painted representations of the human figure followed fixed rules. The whole figure had to be shown. The shoulders were presented frontally, whereas the head, legs, and feet were seen in profile. To achieve the standard proportions between the various parts, a sheet of papyrus was divided into 19 squares. Measuring downward, the head was fitted into the first three rows, the area from the shoulders to the knee into the next ten, and the rest into the remaining six rows.

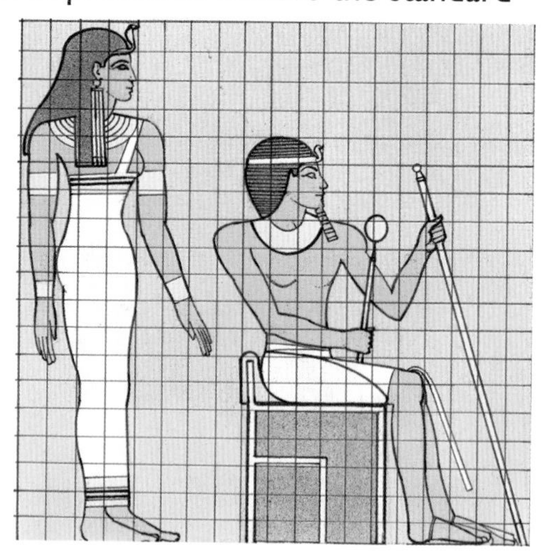

The pyramid of Mycerinus

The third of the Giza pyramids, shown here under construction, was the smallest. Built about 2490 B.C., it is $216^{1}/_{2}$ feet high, with sides $344^{1}/_{2}$ feet long.

The pyramids

The pyramids are undeniable proof of the organizational ability and constructional skills of the ancient Egyptians. These huge objects are tombs, each built to hold the body of a king, whose home it would be throughout eternity. The most important site, containing the three pyramids at Giza, is one of the most famous places in the world.

The pyramid of Cheops
This is the greatest monument in stone ever erected. Constructed around 2550 B.C., it has faces inclined at an angle of 52 degrees; the height is 479 feet and the base measures 754 1/2 feet on each side.

The pyramid of Chephren
This pyramid was built around 2520 B.C. by King Chephren. The face of the Great Sphinx, which stands close to the pyramids, is probably a portrait of the king. The pyramid's height is 469 feet and its base measures 702 feet on each side.

The construction of the pyramids
Experts still argue over exactly what building techniques and which types of ramp were employed to hoist and put into place the enormous blocks of stone. The most plausible theory seems to be that the pyramid was encircled by some kind of ramp that could itself be raised continuously until the apex was reached.

The tomb at Newgrange
c. 3100 B.C., County Meath, Ireland

One of the most important of the megalithic (huge stone) monuments, this belongs to a group of Neolithic tombs in the Boyne Valley It is a passage tomb, with a corridor 60 feet long leading to the burial chamber. There are three subsidiary cells, and the whole structure has a drystone roof, is covered with earth, and is surrounded with a stone curb.

Stonehenge
Monumental stones, placed in a circle or aligned in rows, are among the most extraordinary prehistoric monuments of north western Europe. The stone circle at Stonehenge was built in several phases from about 3000 B.C.

Transportation: a mystery
It is possible that the enormous blocks of stone were pulled on a kind of sled constructed from tree trunks.

Megaliths

The stone architecture of the European Neolithic period is over 6,000 years old. The earliest examples were tombs roofed with capstones (dolmens), and later standing stones, or menhirs, made from long slabs and thrust into the ground.

In honor of the sun's return
On the first day of spring, the rays of the sun filter through gaps between the stones to fall on the "altar-stone" in the center of the complex.

The arrangement
The number of stones and their orientation have been said to correspond to phases of the moon and the position of the sun on the horizon when the seasons change.

Astronomical observatory
Stonehenge was probably a religious center and may also have been an observatory from which the movements of the stars could be studied.

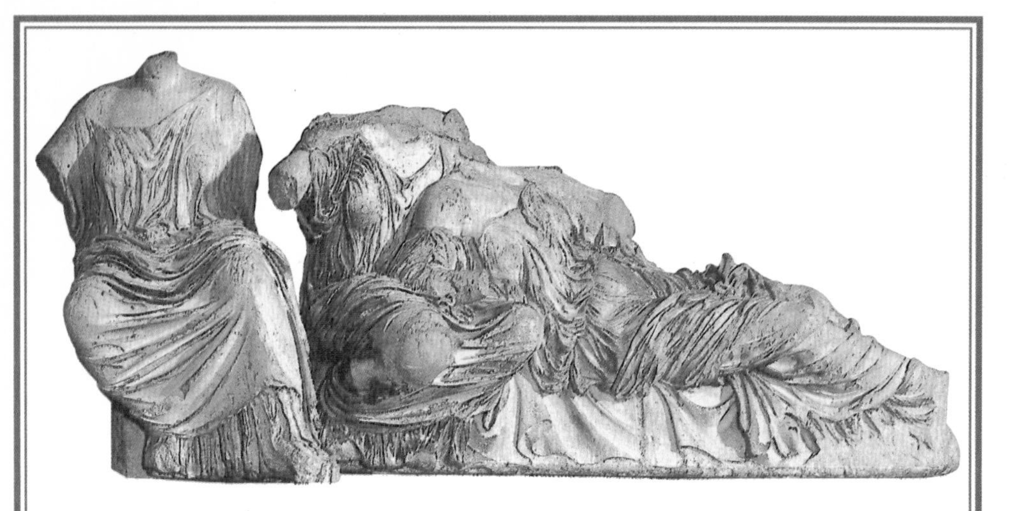

Figures from the east pediment of the Parthenon
Pentelic marble, maximum height 485 ft., 440–432 B.C., British Museum, London

Perhaps by the sculptor Phidias (c. 550–431 B.C.), who directed work on the Parthenon, this group is skillfully composed to fit under the slope of the pediment (the triangular feature over the porch). The figures are part of a group representing the birth of Athena, the patron goddess of Athens. One possibility is that they represent Hestia, goddess of the hearth, and Aphrodite lying in the lap of her mother Dione.

Athens

The Greek city-state of Athens developed an early form of democracy and in the 5th century B.C. played an outstanding part in the war against the Persians. Great artistic advances were also made in Athens, enabling painters and sculptors to represent the human figure far more naturally. During the period when the great Athenian statesman Pericles controlled the government, the Parthenon and other famous temples were constructed on the sacred citadel of Athens, the Acropolis.

Sculptors at work
In Greek art, sculpture and architecture went hand in hand. The temple was the house of the god or goddess, which only the priests were allowed to enter; it was not a place for worship, which took place outside.

Harmony and elegance
The columns, the capitals, and the large triangular pediment above them are the basic constituents of the Greek temple.

The Parthenon
The building was dedicated to Athena the virgin, guardian goddess of the city. The architects were Ictinus and Callicrates.

The frieze
The frieze ran all around the inside of the exterior colonnade. It was 525 feet long and was decorated with splendid reliefs that were originally painted.

Bronze Warrior "A"

Bronze, 6 1/2 ft. high, c. 460–450 B.C., National Archeological Museum, Calabria

In 1972 two ancient statues of warriors, since labeled "A" and "B," were recovered from the sea at Riace, in Calabria, Italy. The statues were being transported from Greece by the ancient Romans and were probably lost in a storm. The bronze shown here is an example of the weight and heroic power typical of such figures. The pose is also characteristic, with most of the weight of the body supported by one of the feet.

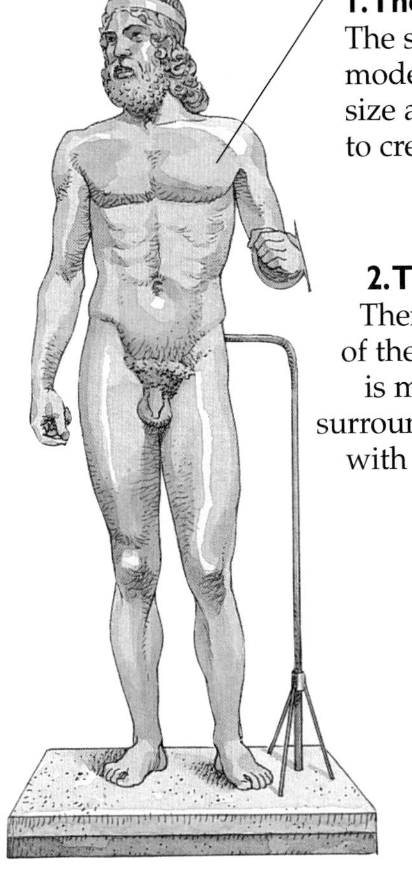

1. The model

The sculptor uses clay to model a statue of the same size as the one he intends to create in bronze.

2. The cast

Then a cast of the model is made by surrounding it with plaster.

6. The channels

Open pipes are attached to the model, ready for bronze to be poured through them.

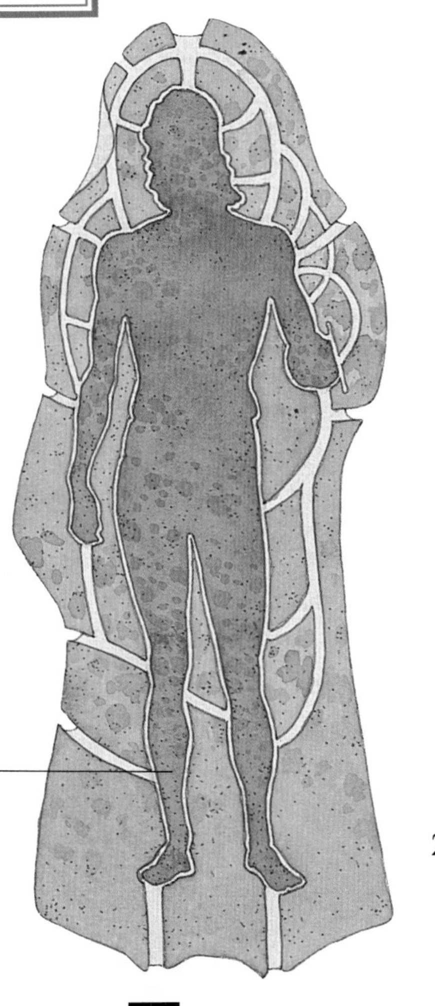

7. The mold for the casting

The model and the pipes are covered with layers of plaster, sand, and cow dung. Great care is taken to keep the pipes unblocked for transmitting wax and bronze.

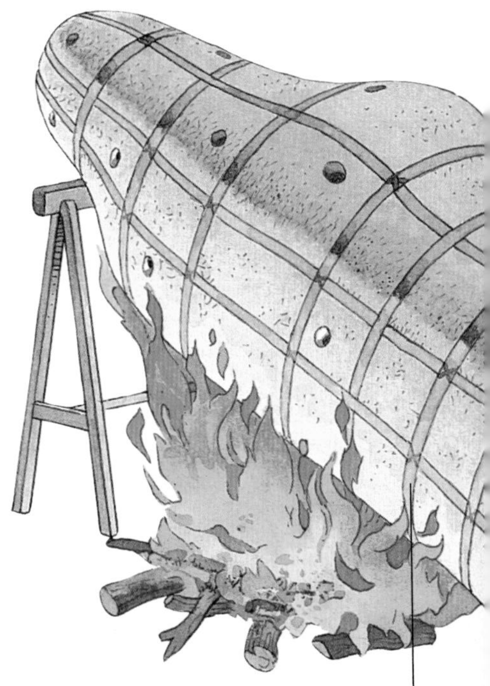

8. Removing the wax

The plaster mold is heated to 200–300 degrees C. This melts the wax, which drains away and leaves a space between the model and the mold.

3. The wax
The surfaces of the cast are covered with a thin layer of wax.

4. The infilling
The cast, strengthened with an iron skeleton (armature), is filled with earth.

Greek sculptors

The sculptors' aim was to represent beauty, which to the Greeks meant harmony, balance, and formal perfection. From the 4th century B.C. to the 1st century A.D. the Greek world produced unsurpassed examples of artistic beauty. Many of their finest marble sculptures are known only in Roman copies, but surviving bronzes enable us to understand Greek casting techniques.

5. The wax model
When the earth has dried out, the plaster is removed to reveal a new model of earth covered with wax.

9. The cast
Bronze is poured into the mold, occupying the space left by the wax.

10. Finishing touches
The bronze figure is freed from the mold and any defects arising from the casting are repaired.

The Pantheon
A.D. 118–128, Rome

Under the Emperor Trajan, the Roman Empire reached its greatest extent. Trajan's successor, Hadrian, was able to devote himself to peaceful activities and became a great builder. One of his outstanding achievements was the Pantheon in Rome, a temple dedicated to all the gods. For the first time, a circular space with a diameter of 141 feet was spanned by a concrete dome which, astonishingly, is still intact. It was the adaptation of this pagan temple to a Christian church in the 7th century A.D. that ensured the building's survival.

Rome

By the 1st century B.C. Rome had conquered an immense empire. Its artistic culture was mainly derived from the Greeks, but the Romans were great builders. Their masterly use of the arch enabled them to construct aqueducts, create large vaults, and raise domes of huge dimensions.

The Colosseum
The most famous ancient Roman building was a vast amphitheater, the Colosseum, built from A.D. 72 to 80. It was designed for spectacles such as gladiatorial contests. Three rows of arches hold up the stands from which spectators viewed events in the arena.

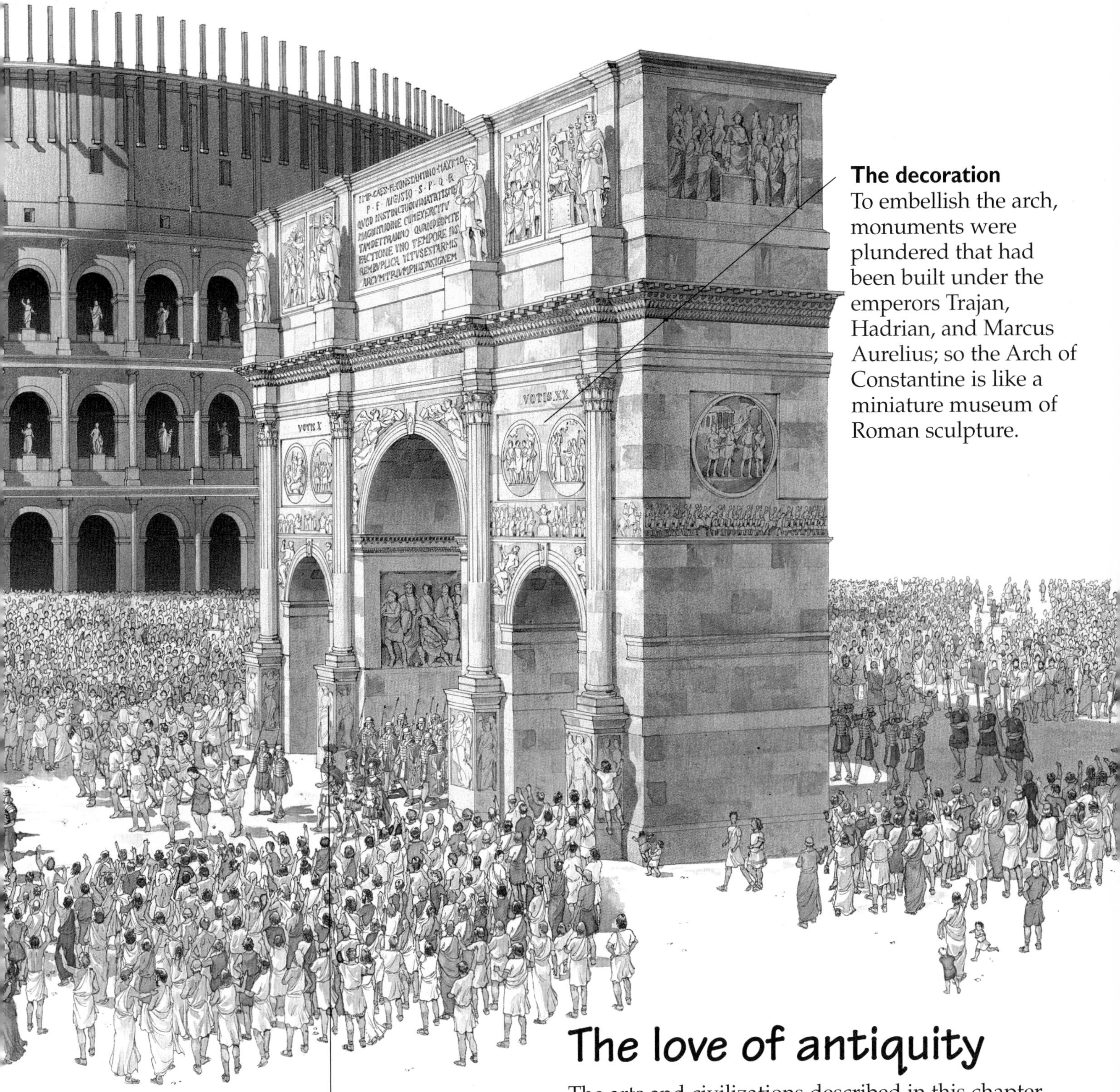

The decoration
To embellish the arch, monuments were plundered that had been built under the emperors Trajan, Hadrian, and Marcus Aurelius; so the Arch of Constantine is like a miniature museum of Roman sculpture.

The Arch of Constantine
The arch was put up in A.D. 316 for the first Christian emperor, Constantine. Like all triumphal arches, it was erected to commemorate Roman military victories. It also provided an imposing setting for the returning army, which paraded through it.

The love of antiquity

The arts and civilizations described in this chapter are very remote in time, but many modern people find them fascinating. The most popular ancient civilization is Egypt, thanks to the pyramids and the discovery of Tutankhamun's tomb. But prehistory has an increasing appeal – so much so that, near the Lascaux cave, now closed because of pollution risks, an imitation cave has been opened for visitors to the site. By contrast with these relatively recent developments, the rediscovery of the Greco-Roman world began over five hundred years ago. Its culture inspired the Renaissance, and art and architecture have drawn on it ever since.

The East

Asia is a huge continent, rich in history because of the great civilizations that have grown up there. The earliest were the empires of Mesopotamia and the cultures of Iran and Anatolia (modern Turkey). Meanwhile, from the 3rd millennium B.C., prehistoric cultures became established along the great rivers of India and China. From then on, Eastern cultures interacted and there were many new developments. Eastern civilizations and their arts were deeply influenced by their great religions – Buddhism, Hinduism, Islam – and by the teachings of Chinese Confucianism.

Relief on the King's Gate at Hattusas.

Our journey

24

26

28

30

32

34

36

In 221 B.C., Shih Huang Di, the first emperor, unified China, linked a series of existing defenses to create the famous Great Wall, and had an extraordinary terracotta army made to guard him in the tomb (pages 24–25). Later, in the 7th century A.D., China became the most powerful empire in the world, while Chinese thought, arts, and customs were affected by Buddhism. (The influence of Buddhism in the East was comparable to that of Christianity on the peoples of the West.) With the spread of Buddhism from China to Japan, much Chinese influence was brought to bear on ancient Japanese culture (pages 26–27). By contrast, in India, the land of its birth, Buddhism was eventually defeated by the people's tenacious devotion to the older religion of Hinduism (pages 28–29). The Hindu religion also spread into Southeast Asia, and in the 10th century it was the faith of the Khmer Empire (pages 30–31). Meanwhile, the religion of Islam was founded by the Prophet Muhammad in the 7th century. It spread throughout the Middle East, along the North African coast, and into Spain, while also penetrating the Indian subcontinent in the 8th century. The Muslim place of worship, the mosque (pages 32–33), was added to the rich variety of Eastern buildings. Painting flowered in China, especially under the Song dynasty (pages 34–35), and printmaking became an art for the masses in 19th-century Japan (pages 36–37).

Anatolia
In the 2nd millennium B.C. the Hittites erected walls with monumental gates in their capital, Hattusas, in Anatolia.

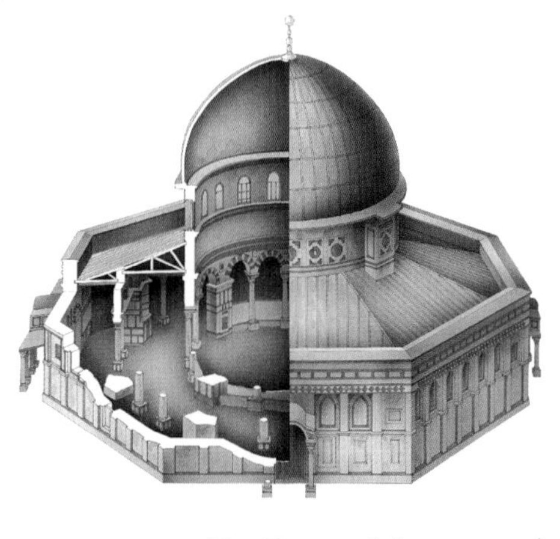

The Dome of the Rock, Jerusalem

The Arabs
Inspired by their new faith in one God, Allah, nomadic tribes swept out of the Arabian peninsula and conquered a vast empire that stretched from Spain to northwest India.

Persia

The Persian Empire reached its height during the 6th and 5th centuries B.C. King Darius built the sumptuous city of Persepolis.

Wall decorations from the palace of Artaxerxes, Susa

Korea

From ancient times painting was important in Korean culture, in the tomb paintings of Koguryo and, later on, in the landscapes of the 12th century.

Korean vase

Japan

Consisting of more than 3,000 islands, Japan was exposed to tidal waves and typhoons. Its culture blended native and Chinese elements.

A mask from the Noh theater

China

In some 3,000 years of history, China alternated between weakness and division and imperial grandeur. China made great contributions to the world in religion, literature, art, and technology.

Song dynasty Buddha, China

The Indian subcontinent

A huge and culturally very rich region, the Indian subcontinent gave birth to several Eastern religions and was later deeply influenced by Islam.

Gupta dynasty Buddha, India

Cambodia

Cambodia was the cradle of the Khmer civilization of the 5th to the 15th century.

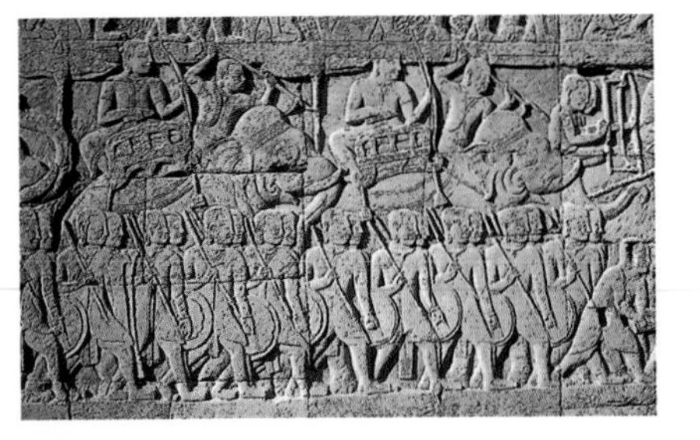

Relief from the Bayon temple at Angkor

Dragon

Bronze, 4th century B.C., Beijing Museum of History

The ancient Chinese were amazingly skillful in the use of bronze-casting techniques. This is evident in the dragon-shaped vessel shown here. It was found in the 4th-century B.C. tomb of a king of Zhongshan. The body of the dragon, inlaid with gold and silver designs, is modeled with full, smooth curves. This treatment was very much to Chinese taste and makes a striking contrast with the thin, sharp teeth that protrude from the creature's mouth.

Xian warriors
The terracotta soldiers were lifesize, and each had facial features different from those of all the others.

Ancient China

Surviving works of art from ancient China include terracottas (baked clay), bronze vessels, objects of carved jade, ivory, and horn, and stone sculptures. In 1974 a sensational archeological find was made in the village of Xian: a terracotta army, made for the emperor who had united China in 221 B.C.

The first emperor
Before his death in 206 B.C., Shih Huang Di built a huge tomb. It was guarded by thousands of terracotta soldiers, horses, and chariots, which were buried in nearby pits.

Attendants after death
In early China, when a king died, his slaves and courtiers were buried alive with him. By Shih Huang Di's time, statues or images of members of the imperial court and other attendants were used instead.

Yakushi (Bhaisajyaguru) Seated
Wood, 19 1/2 in. high, Heian period (9th century), National Museum of Nara

This statue of the healer god Bhaisajyaguru belongs to the first period in which Buddhism spread into Japan. During this phase of its history the newly arrived faith managed to come to terms with Shinto, the long-established religion of Japan. Buddhist theologians interpreted Shinto practices as very ancient versions of Buddhism, in this way reconciling the two faiths.

The spread of Buddhism

Buddhism reached Japan from Korea and China in the 6th century A.D. and strongly influenced the country. For a long time Chinese culture provided models for the Japanese. An example was the establishment in A.D. 710 of a permanent capital at Heijo (present-day Nara), where the Japanese emperor built a temple that demonstrated the imperial government's approval of Buddhism.

The inauguration
The official opening of the temple took place in 752, in the presence of the emperor, the court, and thousands of Buddhist monks who had gathered at Nara from all over Japan.

The temple of Todai-ji
In 741 the Japanese Emperor Shomu ordered the building of the Buddhist temple of Todai-ji in the imperial city of Nara. Many craftsmen were employed to create a colossal statue of the Buddha in a hall in the temple.

A colossal statue
The 52-foot-high statue was made of bronze. According to Japanese tradition, the casting of it used up the country's entire stock of bronze and precious metals.

Shiva Nataraja
Bronze, 19th century, University of Durham Oriental Museum

This small bronze sculpture shows the dance of the god Shiva, who is believed to create and destroy worlds. For some Hindus, such images act as a link between human beings and the gods themselves. Indian artists used traditional symbols such as the circle, standing for the eternal cycle of creation and destruction. The tambourine held by Shiva symbolizes the rhythm of his dance, which is that of the universe itself.

India

Beside the Indus River, at Mohenjo-daro, one of the earliest city-based civilizations developed from the 3rd millennium B.C. Later on, the Indian subcontinent was dominated by the Aryan people. Their religion became the basis of Hinduism, inspiring many art forms. Hinduism is still the dominant religion in the part of the subcontinent occupied by the Republic of India.

Decoration
Outside and inside, a Hindu temple was decorated with vast areas of carvings. Such an abundance of decoration was typical of Indian art.

Hindu temples
At Khajuraho, in the north of India, there is a complex of 20 temples built between 950 and 1050 and dedicated to a variety of gods and goddesses.

The divinity
Inside each of the temples was a shrine where a holy image of the god or goddess was kept.

Southeast Asia

One of the architectural marvels of Asia, Angkor was the capital of the Khmer Empire in Cambodia. It is famous for its huge walls, its temples decorated with superb relief carvings, its lakes and canals, and its wide processional ways lined with splendid sculptures.

Grand entrance
The long processional way served to make pilgrims to Angkor Wat feel awe and devotion as they approached the majestic buildings.

Angkor Wat
A vast royal shrine, Angkor Wat was built by the Khmer kings in the 12th century.

The Churning of the Sea of Milk

Low relief, first half of the 12th century, Angkor Wat, Cambodia

This famous bas-relief (or low relief, not standing out far from the wall) illustrates a Hindu myth in which the gods and demons suspended their eternal conflict and worked together to obtain the elixir of life. The elixir made all who drank it immortal.

Decorations
Besides its grand buildings, the most striking feature of Angkor Wat is the abundance of carving, in the form of reliefs and sculptures.

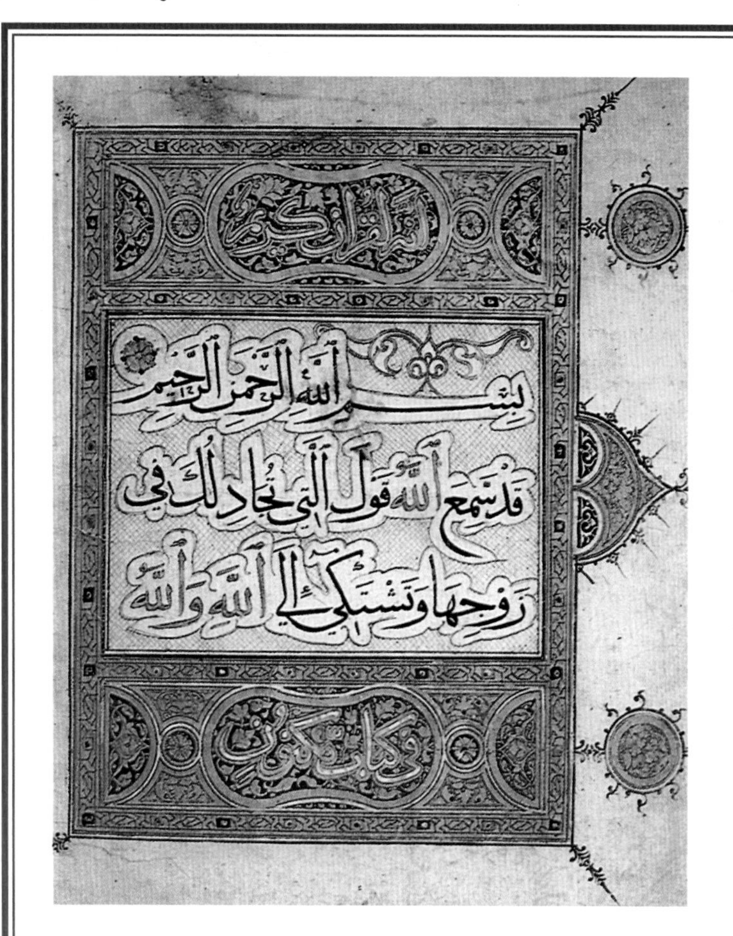

Page of an illuminated Qur'an

Mameluke period (1252–1517), Museum of Atar al-Islamiyya, Kuwait

Muslim craftsmen developed an elaborate decorative art using geometric or plant forms on wall tiles or pottery vessels. These could also be decorated with Arabic calligraphy (writing), usually words or verses from the Qur'an. The beauty of Arabic script can be seen in this illuminated (painted) manuscript.

The minaret
A muezzin, a mosque official, calls Muslims to prayer from the summit of a tower known as a minaret.

Decorations
To decorate mosques, Muslim architects and craftsmen made use of many precious materials.

The Badshahi Mosque
The mosque is at the heart of Muslim religious life. One of the largest mosques in the world is the Badshahi Mosque at Lahore in Pakistan. Its courtyard can hold up to a million pilgrims.

Islam

The Qur'an, the holy book of Islam, forbids artists to make images of God (Allah) or of human beings. Throughout the Islamic world the favored arts have been architecture and elaborate forms of decoration based on geometric and plant forms and the Arabic script.

Bright Weather after a Snowfall on a Mountain Pass

Tang Yin (1470–1524)

Ink and colors on silk, National Museum, Taipei, Taiwan

Tiny figures of some travelers can be seen at the bottom of the painting. They are taking a road that winds steeply through the mountain snows. The trees and distant peaks fade into the misty background which clothes the landscape in a magical light. Like most Chinese painters, Tang Yin was a member of the scholar class and included verses on the upper part of the scroll, written in an elegant script to form part of the composition.

Chinese pottery

The Chinese were skilled potters, famous for their vases and other ceramic objects. They developed porcelain, a fine, hard ware admired all over the world.

Chinese painting

There were Chinese painters even in ancient times, but their works have mostly perished. Court painters were regarded as ordinary craftsmen, but later a great painting tradition arose among Chinese scholar-officials. The art reached its zenith under the Song dynasty (960–1279), but there was another impressive flowering under the Ming (1368–1644).

Scroll paintings
Chinese artists painted hanging scrolls like this one, and also very long hand scrolls, which were slowly unrolled and looked at section by section. In these, the viewer had a sense of making a journey through the landscape.

Silk
Chinese paintings were done on paper, a Chinese invention, or on rolls of silk, known in China since prehistoric times.

Japan

From the 17th to the 19th century, Japan was controlled by the Tokugawa, military dictators who ruled in the name of the emperor. They built splendid tombs for themselves. A popular art, the Japanese print, developed along with the technique of printing in color from wood blocks.

The Impressionist painters
When they came across Japanese prints in Paris, the French Impressionist artists of the 19th century were full of admiration for their pure colors, bold fore shortening (a perspective effect), unusual compositions, and elimination of unnecessary detail.

Discovery
In 1856 Félix Bracquemond, a printmaker in Paris, found that the wrapping paper around some porcelain consisted of beautiful prints unknown in Europe.

Travelers Admiring the Kirifuri Waterfall at the Kurokami Mountain
Katushika Hokusai (1760–1849)
Print from the Shokoku series, c. 1832

The painter and printmaker Hokusai was the most famous Japanese artist of the 18th and 19th centuries. He was also incredibly productive, creating a huge number of notably original and highly imaginative works. In the course of a rich and eventful life he several times changed his style radically and used at least 30 different names on his works. Hokusai executed many series of landscape prints, becoming as famous for them in the West as in his native Japan. He had a marked taste for daring compositions and fantastic or spectacular subjects, as in this waterfall scene from the series "Famous Waterfalls in the Countryside."

The great Asian cultures

The vast size and long history of Asia make it impossible to describe fully the continent's artistic achievements. Long before the ancient Greek and Roman civilizations developed in Europe, India and China were producing distinctive arts. Iranian traditions, too, were remarkably long-lived, lasting in various forms into the Middle Ages. By then, Islamic art was spreading through the Mediterranean and in Asia and Africa, while societies from Turkey to Java were flourishing at high cultural levels. Eruptions of new peoples from Central Asia, though destructive at first, also enriched the cultural scene, among other things giving Islam a more regionally varied and multilingual aspect. Meanwhile, the high civilizations of the Far East, later to influence European art so deeply, continued to develop in fascinating ways.

Christian Art

In the 4th century A.D., Christianity became the religion of the Roman Empire. Soon, the eastern half of the Empire became known as Byzantium, and the Church there adopted the Greek language and culture. The western part of the Empire collapsed, but the Latin-based Church survived and became a dominant force in western Europe by converting barbarian peoples. Two distinct artistic languages emerged. In the East, Byzantine art began its long history. In the West, after centuries of tumult, the 11th century saw a great revival in architecture, sculpture, and painting.

Our journey

40

42

44

46

48

50

In the 6th century A.D. the political center of the Mediterranean was Constantinople (modern Istanbul, Turkey). It was the capital of the East Roman (later the Byzantine) Empire. Under the Emperor Justinian, Byzantine art flourished; the magnificent church of Santa Sophia was built in Constantinople, and superb mosaics were made at Ravenna, a Byzantine outpost in Italy (pages 40–41). After the collapse of the Roman Empire in the West, much of Europe was briefly united under Charlemagne in the 9th century, and there was a partial artistic reawakening. But a much greater cultural revival took place in the West after the year 1000, when population rose, agriculture expanded, trading contacts were renewed, and the Church assumed a dominant position in medieval society. Many churches and cathedrals were built, and in little more than a hundred years the monumental Romanesque style (pages 42–43) gave way to the soaring Gothic (pages 44–45). There was also a renewed interest in naturalistic representation and secular subjects reentered art. Nevertheless, mosaic remained the dominant mode of religious decoration, even in the West, until the 12th century (pages 46–47). Then sacred subjects were shown in great frescoes (wall paintings) in churches (pages 48–49) and also on wood panels (pages 50–51). In both fields the Italian painter Giotto was the supreme genius, pioneering a new kind of Western art.

The nave of Durham Cathedral

England

England was occupied by the Romans until the early 5th century. After the Romans left, it was conquered first by the Anglo-Saxons and then, in 1066, by William of Normandy. The Normans brought in the Romanesque architectural style, often known as Norman.

Figures from Chartres Cathedral

France

Throughout medieval times France was the heart of Europe. In the 9th century it was part of the cultural rebirth under Charlemagne. The late 13th century saw the flowering of great French cathedrals and Gothic sculpture.

Spain

Most of the Iberian peninsula was conquered by Muslim Arabs in the 8th century. From the early 11th century, small Christian states in the north began to drive back the Muslims.

Alhambra Palace at Granada

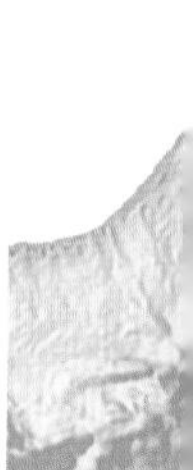

Section of Florence Baptistery

Florence

The greatest financial and commercial center in Europe, Florence was the native city of Giotto, a painter of splendid drama and realism whose works looked forward to the birth of the Renaissance.

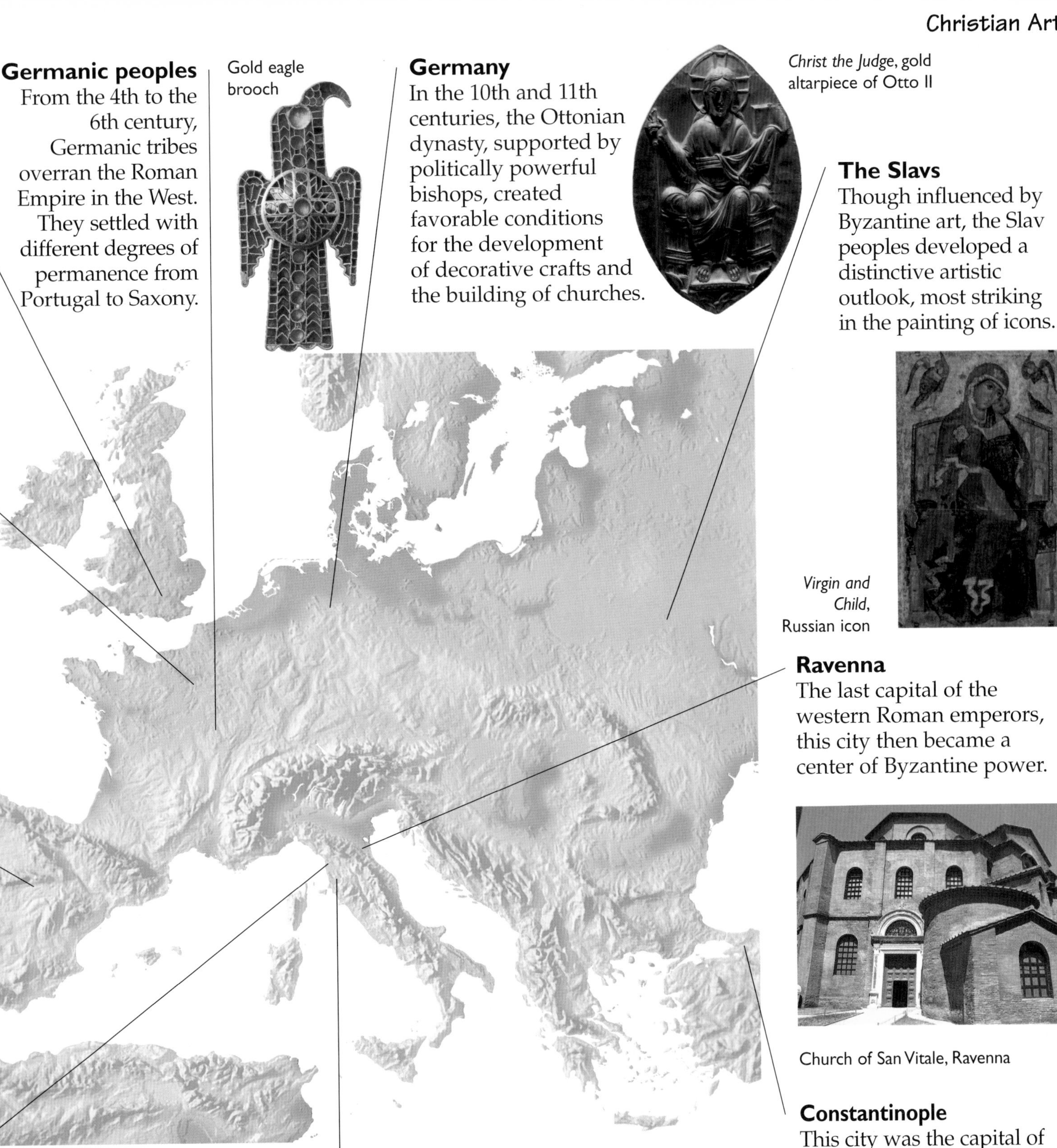

Germanic peoples

From the 4th to the 6th century, Germanic tribes overran the Roman Empire in the West. They settled with different degrees of permanence from Portugal to Saxony.

Gold eagle brooch

Germany

In the 10th and 11th centuries, the Ottonian dynasty, supported by politically powerful bishops, created favorable conditions for the development of decorative crafts and the building of churches.

Christ the Judge, gold altarpiece of Otto II

The Slavs

Though influenced by Byzantine art, the Slav peoples developed a distinctive artistic outlook, most striking in the painting of icons.

Virgin and Child, Russian icon

Ravenna

The last capital of the western Roman emperors, this city then became a center of Byzantine power.

Church of San Vitale, Ravenna

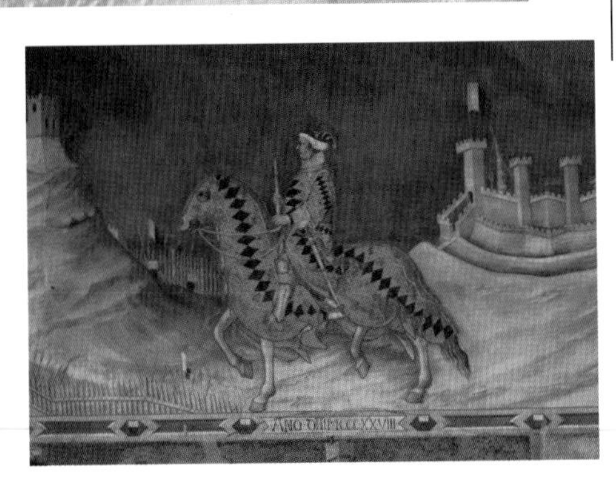

Simone Martini, *Guidoriccio da Fogliano*

Siena

A virtually independent city, Siena was the great rival of Florence. Flourishing through commercial activity, it boasted a particularly refined school of artists.

Interior of Santa Sophia, Istanbul

Constantinople

This city was the capital of the Roman Empire in the East (known in its medieval form as Byzantium). It survived the barbarian invasions, and, while post-Roman Europe became impoverished, Byzantium remained formidable and Constantinople was the greatest city in Christendom.

Justinian and His Court
Wall mosaic, 546–47, church of San Vitale, Ravenna, Italy

Under the Emperor Justinian, the Byzantines temporarily reconquered Italy and made Ravenna their capital in the peninsula. The apse of the church of San Vitale in Ravenna was decorated with images of Justinian and his empress, Theodora. In this group of mosaics, the figures are shown in conventional, near-identical poses, and only the faces are individualized. The drapery, though stylized, has some relation to the older Greek radition. Colors are used symbolically; for example, the halo round the emperor's head is silver, indicating his high rank.

Byzantine art

The Byzantine Empire was Greek in language and culture, and its art displayed characteristics carried over from Greek and Roman times, for example the treatment of drapery and the use of mosaics. But the strict conventions and fixed imagery of Byzantine art limited the artist's freedom and made any form of realism impossible.

Santa Sophia
Between 532 and 537, Justinian rebuilt the church that had stood on this spot, which was dedicated to wisdom ("sophia" in Greek). Justinian's huge creation later became a mosque, and it is now a museum.

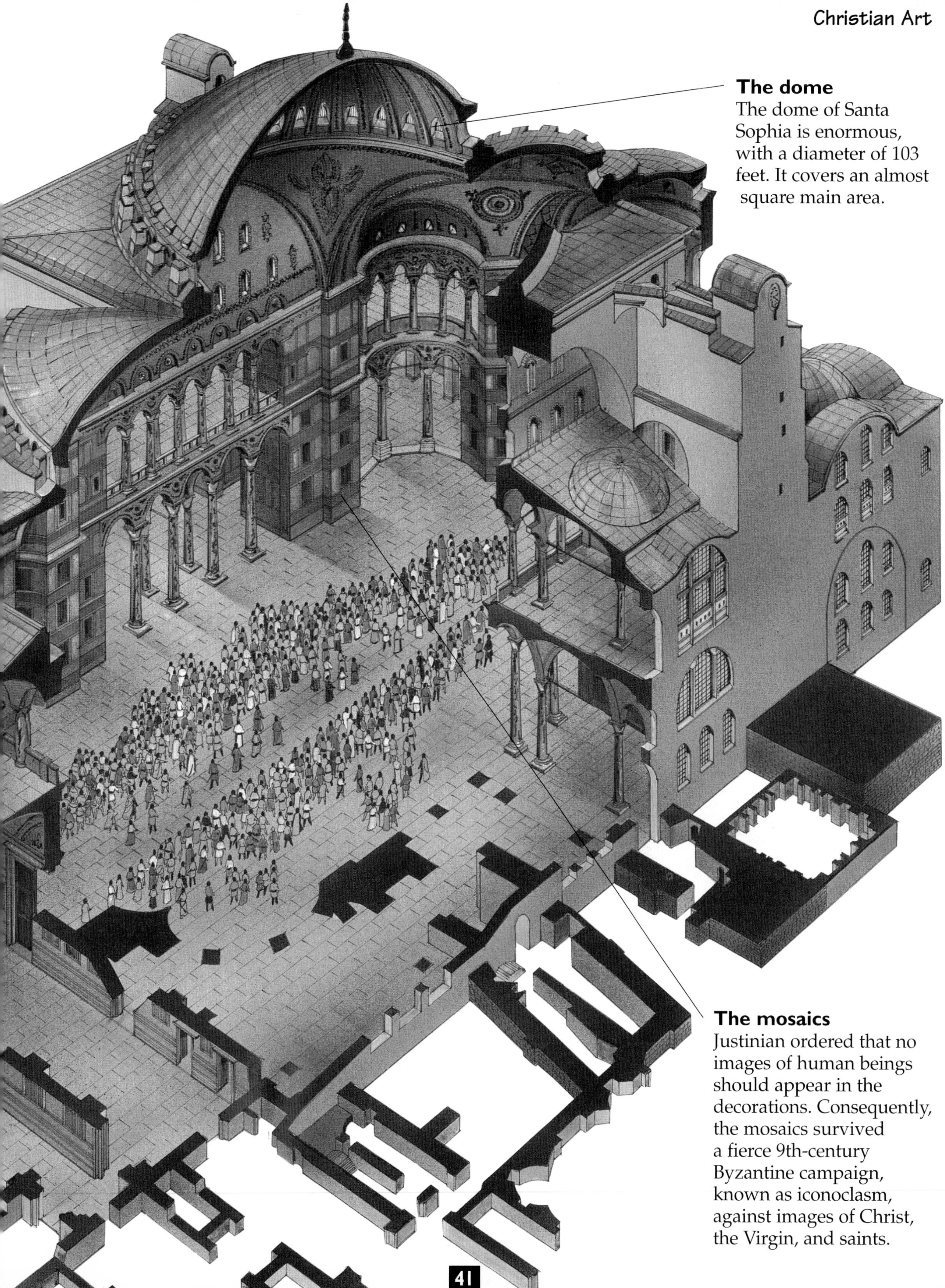

The dome
The dome of Santa Sophia is enormous, with a diameter of 103 feet. It covers an almost square main area.

The mosaics
Justinian ordered that no images of human beings should appear in the decorations. Consequently, the mosaics survived a fierce 9th-century Byzantine campaign, known as iconoclasm, against images of Christ, the Virgin, and saints.

Durham
The cathedral of this city in northeast England was built between 1083 and 1183.

Romanesque

From about A.D. 1000, in towns and villages all over Europe, religious buildings were being constructed, or reconstructed, in stone. Giving visible form to the authority of the Church, they towered over the houses around them, almost all of which were made of wood. These Romanesque structures, with their characteristic round arches, were supported by massive pillars, thick walls, and buttresses (blocks of masonry).

The cathedral
The word "cathedral" means the site of a bishop's throne (in Latin, "cathedra"). So, in practice, a cathedral is usually the grandest church in the area ruled by a bishop. Medieval cathedrals were funded by the people, who contributed labor and money to obtain forgiveness for their sins.

The plan
Romanesque churches took the form of a Latin cross (with one arm longer than the other three). The relatively short transepts separated the long central area (the nave) from the chancel, which was reserved for the clergy.

The Last Judgment
Gislebertus (12th century)
1120–35, cathedral of St. Lazare, Autun, France

At the entrance of Romanesque churches, the tympanum (the area over the porch) was crowded with sculpted figures. Such figures served to convey Christian teachings, when many people could not read. Here, Christ sits in judgment with the saved on his right hand and the damned cast out on his other side.

Gothic arches
These pointed arches are stronger and more flexible than round ones. They strengthen the impression that the cathedral is reaching toward the sky.

The Founders
Master of Naumburg (13th century)
c. 1260, Naumburg Cathedral, Germany

After the collapse of the classical Greek and Roman world, no large stone sculpture was created until about the mid-12th century. Then great column-figures were made to stand on the façades of cathedrals. Within a few decades, sculpture in the round (completely detached from the wall behind) appeared once more in Europe. Gradually the poses became more natural. Here, in depicting Eckehardt and Uta, the founders of Naumburg Cathedral, the sculptor clearly worked from real models.

The Church triumphant
Architects, sculptors, glassworkers, and decorators created huge, high buildings, whose beauty was enhanced inside by the play of light and shade. By this time the Church was a powerful international institution as well as a spiritual force.

Gothic

It was discovered by trial and error that the weight of a vault could be supported by thin ribs running from the roof and down the pillars to the floor. The walls no longer had to be very thick, and because they were not load-bearing, large areas could be left unfilled and used for windows. Now soaring, light-filled cathedrals could be built.

Flying buttresses
These support the outside of the cathedral, taking the thrust from the upper story and transferring it to the masonry below; their curved shapes minimize any interference with the window areas.

Two mosaics
Workshop of Meliore (early 13th century)
Workshop of Cimabue (later 13th century)
Baptistery of San Giovanni, Florence, Italy

The beautiful 11th-century baptistery of San Giovanni stands in the center of Florence. The mosaics in the vault show how ways of representing people changed in the course of the 13th century. The figure of Christ the Judge (above) is static and stylized; the faces of the bystanders (below), from later in the century, are more expressive, and there is a sense of movement in the grouping of the figures.

Mosaics

Mosaics provided a striking and durable form of decoration, which was used in churches until the 13th century. Mosaics were ancient in origin (Greco-Roman and Byzantine), but an important new technique was developed during the Middle Ages. Examples of old and new techniques are found in the church of Santa Maria in Trastevere, Rome, the setting for the main illustration.

The medieval technique:
1. A mosaic is made from little pieces of colored glass or stone, called tesserae. The new technique in medieval times was to arrange the tesserae on a panel, then cover them with a strong piece of canvas coated with a soluble glue.

2. The canvas
With the mosaic adhering to it, the canvas was rolled up and hoisted onto the scaffolding.

The ancient technique
The vault of the apse is decorated with a 12th-century mosaic. This was created in the traditional way: pressing the tesserae directly into plaster that is still damp.

3. Put into place
The canvas was unrolled and pressed flat against a wall that had been covered with fresh plaster so that the tesserae would stick into it.

4. Revealed
Once the plaster had dried, the canvas was soaked and peeled away from the mosaic.

1. The sinopia
The walls were covered with a plaster base (the arriccio), on which the painter outlined the work in red chalk; this drawing was known as the sinopia.

2. The intonaco
An assistant spread a layer of fresh plaster (the intonaco) over the part of the sinopia that was to be painted in the course of the day.

3. The giornata
The giornata (day-piece) was the area to be painted in the course of the day. It was harder to paint detail at the necessary speed than broad colored areas.

Pigments
The pigments were derived from animal, mineral, or vegetable sources. Painting was done from the top.

Fresco

This very ancient technique of wall painting was revived in the 13th and 14th centuries, especially in Italy. The painter worked directly onto a damp plaster surface, so that pigments and plaster bonded as they dried. The painter had to work fast, before the plaster dried.

Paintings of religious stories, architecture, and abstract decoration cover the walls and ceiling.

The Gift of the Cloak

Giotto di Bondone (c. 1265–1337)
Fresco, c. 1290–95, Basilica of St. Francis, Assisi

The church at Assisi is the center of the Franciscan order, which was founded by Saint Francis. It is a double church (one placed above the other), and many artists were employed in its decoration. Not all art historians believe that the 28-fresco cycle of the life of Saint Francis was painted by Giotto, but the scenes are depicted in his realistic style. It was Giotto, who, after 1,000 years of non-realistic, symbolic art, refound the art of painting on a flat surface to give the illusion of three-dimensional reality.

Painting on a panel

Painting on wooden panels was another ancient technique that became widely used in the 13th century. The panels took various forms, including the one shown here: a large cross, intended for an altar or the center of a church, at the meeting point between the clergy and the congregation. The preparatory work was carried out by a team of assistants in the workshop of a master craftsman.

Preparatory work
It took many days to complete all the stages of getting a large wooden panel ready for painting.

1. Sizing
Three coats of glue were spread over the entire panel and frame.

2. Cloth base
The panel was covered with thin strips of linen cloth impregnated with glue.

3. Plastering
When the glue was dry, two layers of plaster were spread over the panel.

4. Drying
Before anything else could be done, the plaster had to be left to dry out.

5. Smoothing
The plaster was scraped until the surface was smooth and polished.

8. Gilding
Some parts of the panel and the cross were gilded, heightening the sumptuous effect.

9. Finishing the job
The final stages of the work were carried out with the cross in an upright position.

Maestà

Duccio di Buoninsegna (active from 1278; died before 1310)

Tempera on panel, 1311, Museo dell'Opera del Duomo, Siena

Both sides of this panel are painted. The front (above) shows the Virgin in Majesty, seated with her child in her arms and surrounded by saints and angels. The other side of the panel relates the Passion of Christ. While Giotto was introducing a new realism into Italian art, this splendid panel painting, executed for the altar of Siena's cathedral, is a supreme example of the decorative quality that appealed to medieval taste. The painting of the Crucifixion (right) is part of the back of the panel.

6. The outline
The artist sketched the design in charcoal, then outlined it in thin ink.

7. Bole
Bole was a specially imported reddish clay. It was mixed with egg white and used as a base for gilding.

The glory of medieval art

The seven episodes described in this part of our journey (pages 38–51) belong to the era known in the West as the Middle Ages. This was once looked upon as a barren period between the wonders of classical civilization and the 15th-century Renaissance, which saw itself as, among other things, a revival of classical values. The medieval arts certainly violated classical ideas, such as the realistic representation of natural appearances and spatial relationships. But this was because the artistic language used from the 4th to the 14th centuries had other expressive or symbolic aims, such as inducing feelings of religious awe, and these were triumphantly achieved.

The New World

About 50,000 years ago, during the last Ice Age, small groups of hunters crossed the Bering Strait and reached Alaska. From there, over the centuries, they spread as far as Tierra del Fuego. Great civilizations developed in Central America, the best known being those of the Maya and the Aztecs. Farther south, in Peru, the Incas built up a powerful state, while the cultures that arose in North America were less advanced in technology and organization. At the end of the 15th century, the ways of life of all these civilizations were disrupted by the arrival of Europeans, who triumphed by force of arms and began a long destructive process that almost wiped out the native American peoples and their cultures.

Our journey

54

56

58

60

Maya civilization was perhaps the most fascinating of the many cultures that grew up in Central America; it covered the southern part of Mexico, Guatemala, El Salvador, and parts of Honduras and Nicaragua. The Maya produced some of the finest examples of pre-Columbian (pre-European) art, notably the awe-inspiring ceremonial areas of the cities (pages 54–55). Mayan knowledge of the techniques of architecture was exceptionally developed. The Andean region of South America also produced many societies over a long period, starting with the advanced cultures of the Mochica (pages 56–57) and Chimú. The final phase, in the 16th century, was marked by the brief supremacy of the Inca Empire; the achievements of its engineers were matched by those of its craftsmen, who excelled in arts such as goldworking and weaving. In North America, from about 300 B.C., the Hohokam and Mogollon peoples started to create fairly large settlements and develop agriculture and methods of irrigation. Later the Anasazi were also highly creative, and around A.D. 1000, they developed an original type of large village (pages 58–59). The great civilizations of Central and South America also produced art forms that their European conquerors failed to notice or were unable to appreciate. Among these was the art of featherwork, practiced with particular skill by the Maya and the Aztecs (pages 60–61).

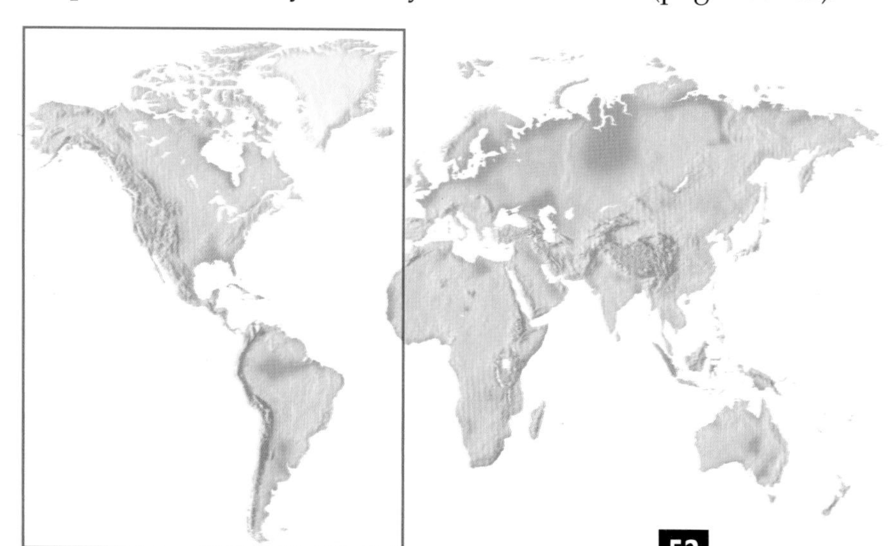

Indians of the Northwest
From the Californian coast to Alaska, Indian tribes lived by fishing and dwelt in wooden houses. Some tribes in the far Northwest put up totem poles, tall wooden structures with elaborate carved heads and creatures on them.

Nootka mask

Indians of the Southwest
A culture developed in the Southwest around A.D. 1000, whose people dwelt in stone-built villages and lived by growing corn.

Anasazi pottery

The Aztecs
From humble beginnings in the 12th century, the Aztecs built up a powerful empire in northern Mexico. They took over building techniques and knowledge of astronomy, art, and religion from the Maya and Toltec cultures.

Toltec mask

The Plains Indians

As early as the 2nd millennium B.C., the life of the Plains Indians was based on hunting buffalo. These provided food, skins, and shelter (tents).

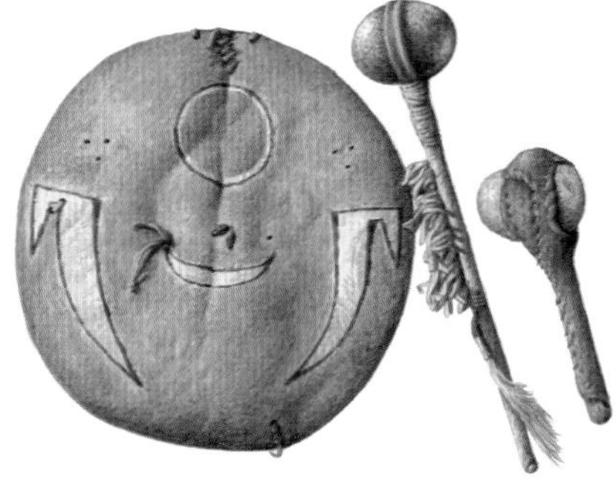

Shield and weapons of the Cree Indians

The Maya

Mainly occupying southern Mexico, the Maya world was divided into city-states. From the 3rd to the 10th century this was an advanced civilization, especially knowledgeable in astronomy and mathematics.

Mayan relief

The Amazon

In the Amazon basin, the Indian inhabitants were above all fisherfolk and craftsmen, especially in working gold.

Amazonian Indian

Mochica portrait vessel

Andean cultures

From the 2nd century B.C., advanced cultures developed on the slopes of the great Andean mountain chain. They were notable for their work as potters and weavers.

The Incas

The new imperial power of the Incas was consolidated in the 15th century. All parts of their vast empire were bound together by an advanced communications network. The emperor was absolute ruler.

Inca embroidered fabric

Mayan fresco
8th century A.D., Bonampak

A cycle of vivid paintings, still in good condition, was discovered on a wall in a palace in the Mayan city of Bonampak. The paintings date back to the 8th century and celebrate a Mayan victory in battle. Soldiers are shown marching in file, but there is also a scene (above) in which Maya warriors are attacking their enemies. The unknown Maya artist displayed great skill in picturing action. None of the warriors appears in a stiff or static pose, and in most cases they are shown leaning forward as they thrust with their spears.

The Maya

Masterpieces of architecture were created for the ceremonial area of a Mayan city, where religious rites were celebrated. Nothing was left to chance: the great stepped pyramids, the palaces, the large open squares, and the altars were part of an overall design, carefully thought out and carried through with great accuracy.

Copan
The city of Copan in Honduras was an important center of Mayan astronomy. Study of the stars and planets was, with mathematics, the science that most interested the Maya.

Temples
Only priests were allowed to enter the temples – small structures standing on huge stepped pyramids.

Ceremonies
Ordinary people gathered at the foot of sacred buildings for religious ceremonies. Some of these involved human sacrifices.

Andean civilization

In the central region of the great Andean mountain chain of South America, conditions are very hostile. Surprisingly, it was here that one of the most advanced American civilizations grew up; and in fact there is evidence of cultural activity in the area as far back as 1000 B.C.

A chief's tomb
In 1988, near the pyramid of Sipan, an important discovery was made: the tomb of a Mochica chief containing many precious objects.

Buried with his wives and warriors
Buried around the chief were the bodies of warrior-priests and women. These have had their feet cut off, perhaps to symbolize their dependence on their lord.

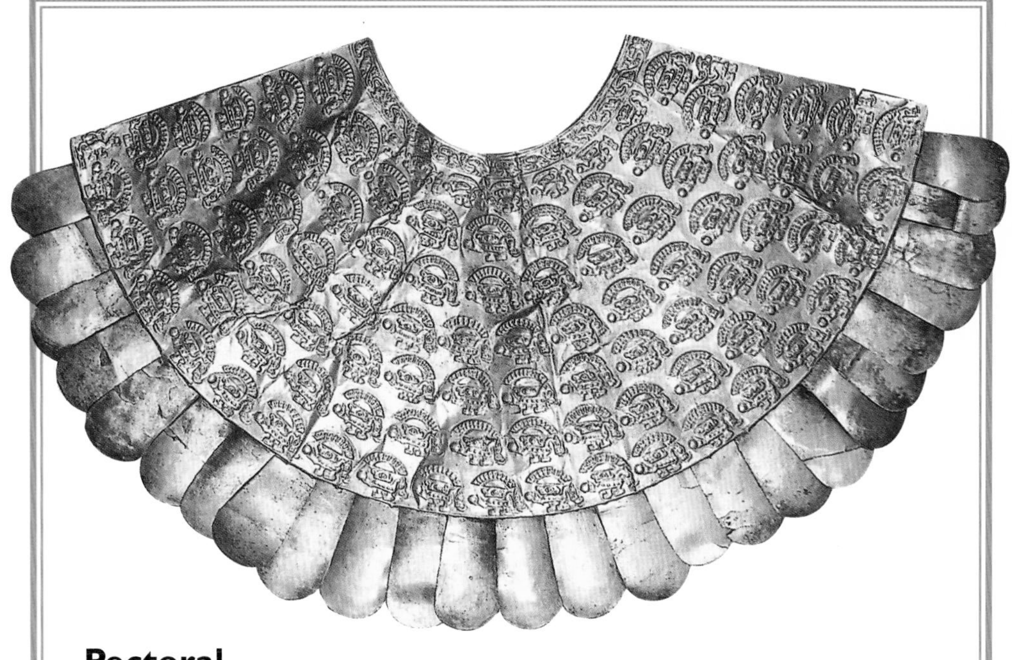

Pectoral

Chimú culture, recent Intermediate period (A.D. 1000–1450)

Embossed gold, 8 in. high, 19 in. diameter, Larco Herrera Museum, Lima

Inca nobles wore decorated collars, also known as pectorals. Craftsmen made these as rich as possible, above all in gold. The techniques they used were inherited from the previous Andean culture, that of the Chimú, who were defeated by the Incas in the 15th century. The gold and silver used by Inca craftsmen were the exclusive property of the emperor. He was the political and religious leader of the largest American empire before Europeans reached the New World.

A rich hoard

Many beautifully decorated objects were placed in the grave with a Mochica chief. This tomb contains hair ornaments, gold plates to cover the body, a fine collar, ornaments of gold, silver, and copper, a gold bell, bracelets, and daggers.

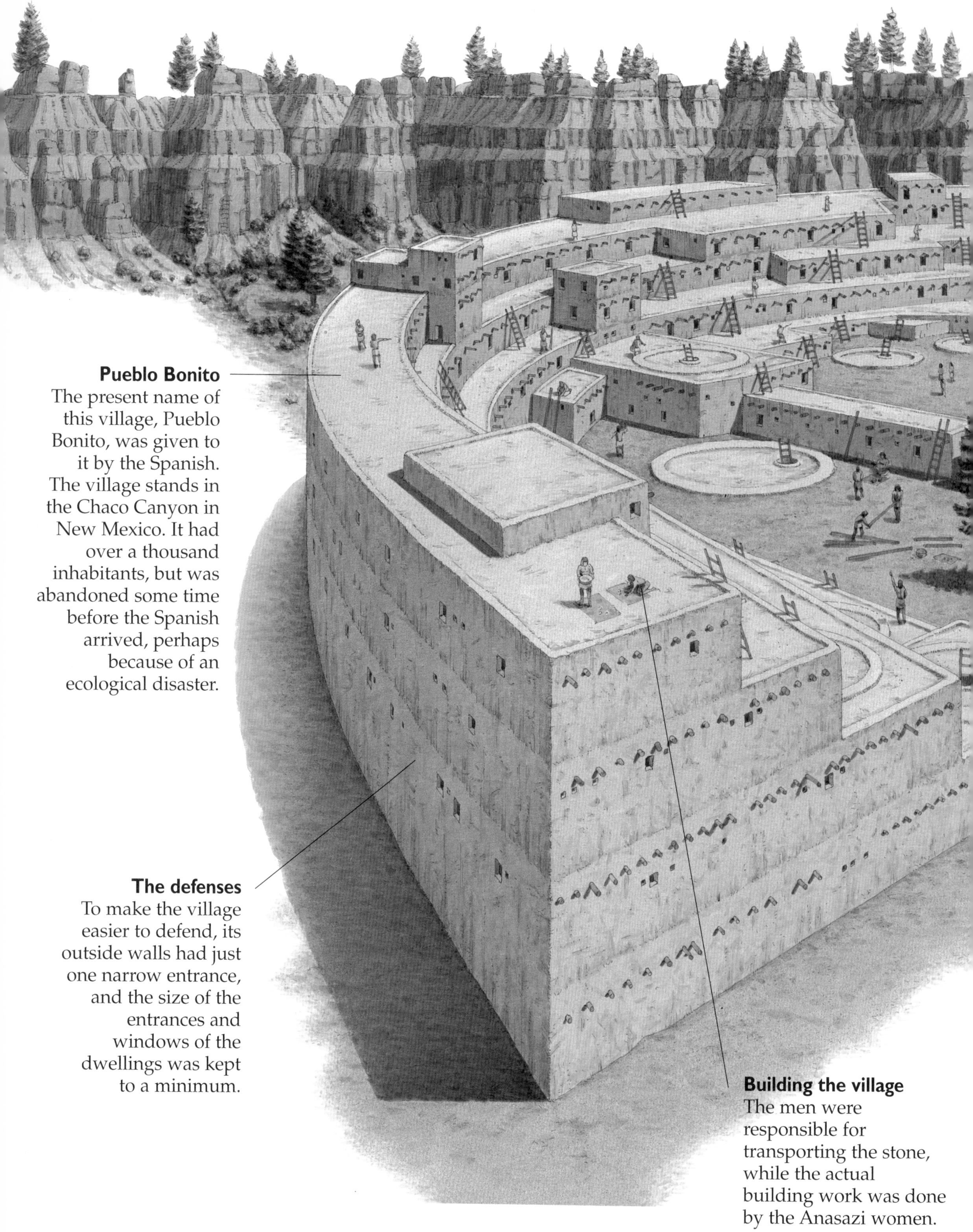

Pueblo Bonito
The present name of this village, Pueblo Bonito, was given to it by the Spanish. The village stands in the Chaco Canyon in New Mexico. It had over a thousand inhabitants, but was abandoned some time before the Spanish arrived, perhaps because of an ecological disaster.

The defenses
To make the village easier to defend, its outside walls had just one narrow entrance, and the size of the entrances and windows of the dwellings was kept to a minimum.

Building the village
The men were responsible for transporting the stone, while the actual building work was done by the Anasazi women.

The Anasazi

Between A.D. 100 and 1300, the people of this culture built large, stone-walled villages in the arid terrain of New Mexico, Arizona, and Colorado. Standing in rocky canyons, the villages were astonishing structures with houses up to four floors high and underground rooms.

The kiva
This was the name of an underground room. Secret rites were performed there, and it was also where the leading men of the village made important decisions.

Wingate black-on-red jar

Anasazi

Ceramic, 13 in. diameter, 1000-1200, Arizona or New Mexico, Dallas Museum of Art

Except for basketmaking, painted pottery was the Anasazi's most important form of art. Their vessels were made without using a potter's wheel, which they had not discovered. They decorated them with geometric designs or human figures and stylized animals; the colors were made with minerals, and chewed-up yucca leaves served as paintbrushes. Pottery was used for everyday purposes, in ceremonies, and as a means of exchange. The Hopi, who are descendants of the Anasazi, produce painted pottery of a similar type.

Calendar stone
Carved stone, weighing about 25 tons, and $11^{3/4}$ ft. diameter, 1479, Museum of Anthropology, Mexico City

When the Aztec Empire was at its height, the religious leaders placed this huge stone in the sacred enclosure at Tenochtitlan. The carvings on the stone summarized many of the Aztecs' beliefs about the creation of the world and the meaning of time. The stone was in fact a calendar, filled with complex symbolic images. In the center, the sun god is shown with his tongue hanging out of his mouth, as if to remind the Aztecs that he thirsted for blood and that it was their duty to feed him by making human sacrifices. Around the sun god are symbols of the four suns believed to have existed in previous ages; according to Aztec mythology there had been four earlier periods of history, each ending in a catastrophic event. In the circular band around the suns are symbols of the twenty days that made up the months of a solar year. The outermost circle consists of the bodies of two large serpents that symbolize time itself.

The headdress
The headdress was made with the brilliantly colored feathers of the quetzal, a bird regarded as sacred by the Aztecs. Once they had plucked it, they released it back into the wild.

A gift
In 1519 the Aztec Emperor Montezuma presented a magnificent headdress to Cortes, leader of the Spanish expedition to Mexico that was to destroy the Aztecs

The Aztecs

Skillful builders and sculptors, the Aztecs also excelled in featherwork, making superb plumed headdresses for the nobility. The craftsmen who worked in precious metals came to be known as toltecs ("well made").

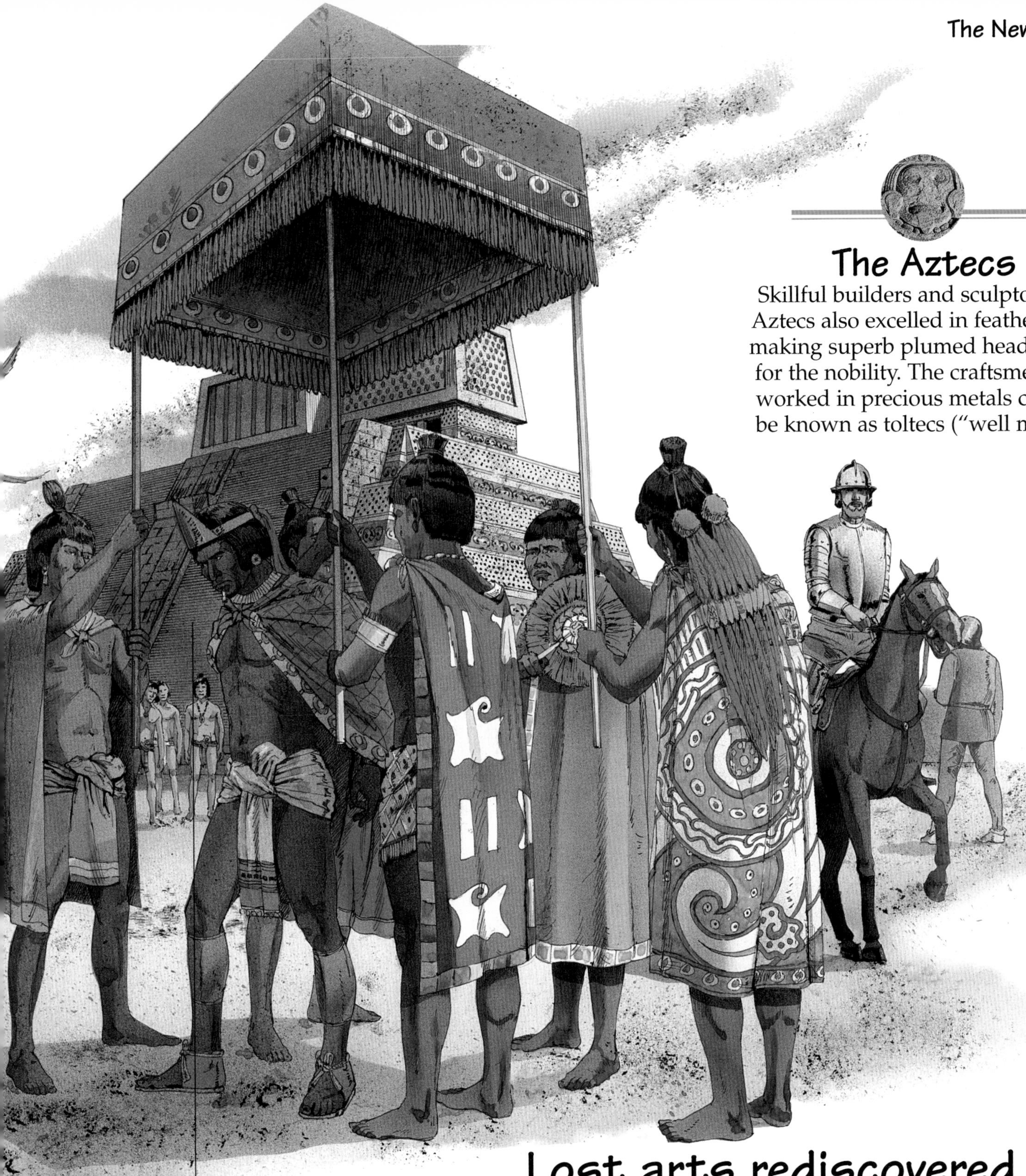

Lost arts rediscovered

For a long time, Amerindian arts were appreciated only by archeologists. They were unknown to the wider world because their makers were geographically isolated and their cultures had been brutally suppressed by European invaders. But in time evidence emerged of the cultures of Mexico, Central America, and the central Andean region. The colossal stone heads of the Olmecs displayed an advanced sculptural technique. During the 16th century, gold objects found in Colombia triggered the myth of Eldorado. Other fascinating discoveries included the wall paintings of Bonampak, the temples of Guatemala, and the remains of Tenochtitlan.

Tenochtitlan
The capital of the Aztec Empire, Tenochtitlan was a city of canals and stepped pyramids.

The Renaissance

The Renaissance is the term used to describe the new European attitudes and values that replaced the medieval worldview. These first appeared in Italy in about 1400, spreading much later to the rest of Europe. In Italy, a new awareness of the achievements of ancient Greece and Rome sparked developments in art and literature and a break with the otherworldly outlook of the Middle Ages; the Renaissance attitude was that "man can do all things." Renaissance art, however, owed much to developments in Flanders as well as to a succession of great Italian painters and sculptors.

Our journey

Adopting different ideals from those of the Middle Ages, Renaissance artists aimed to represent human realities and to capture the appearance of nature. In this quest for realism, painters in Florence made a discovery of decisive importance: the laws of perspective (pages 64–65), which provided mathematical rules enabling artists to achieve an illusion of depth when painting or drawing on a flat surface. This was soon combined with the practice, typical of Flemish artists (pages 66–67), of recording people and their surroundings with great accuracy. The new art flourished in the workshops of Florence (pages 68–69). A brief period in the late 15th and early 16th centuries is known as the High Renaissance, because it was then that the search for harmony, balance, and ideal beauty reached its climax in the work of three supreme artists: Leonardo (pages 70–71), Michelangelo (pages 72–73), and Raphael (pages 74–75). Rome was the main center of the High Renaissance, but there were important developments in many other parts of Italy. The wealthy Venetian Republic (pages 76–77) gave rise to a school of great colorists working in the medium of oil painting. Renaissance ideas gradually spread to other parts of Europe, finding particularly gifted interpreters in Germany (pages 78–79).

64

66

68

70

72

74

76

78

England
Renaissance art entered England via the court of Henry VIII. Portraiture was appreciated, but was also used for political purposes.

Holbein, *Portrait of Henry VIII*

France
France's wars led to direct contact with Italy. Chateaus were built, Leonardo became the king's guest, and Italian artists founded the school of Fontainebleau.

Chateau of Chambord

Spain
During the reigns of Charles V and his son Philip II, Spain became a great power and produced some important artists.

Ship in which Magellan sailed around the world

Flanders
Flanders was the main industrial and commercial region in northern Europe, and also important as an art center.

Bruegel, *Children's Games*

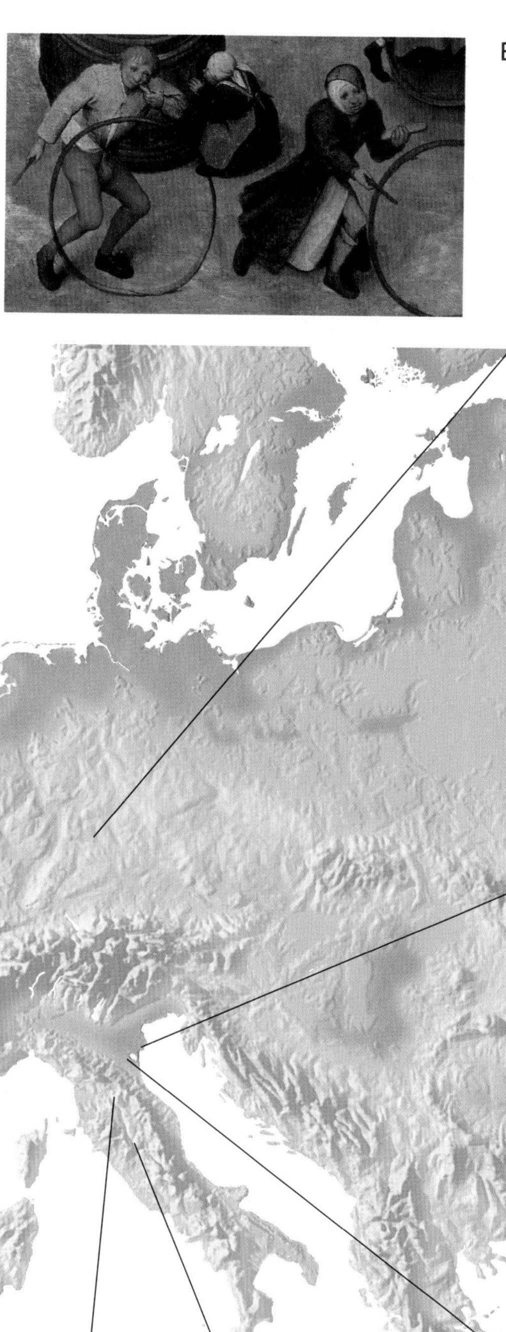

Germany
Divided into many states, Germany had a great woodcarving tradition. By the early 16th century it was also producing great painters.

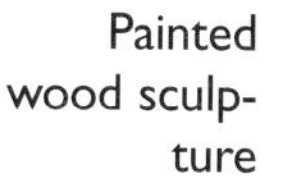
Painted wood sculpture

Venice
The splendid history of this commercial and maritime power now reached its peak.

Titian, *Self-portrait*

Brunelleschi, Dome of Florence Cathedral

Florence
A great commercial center, Florence was the birthplace of the Renaissance and of many great artists.

Rome
Around 1500, thanks to the popes, Rome replaced Florence as the major art center.

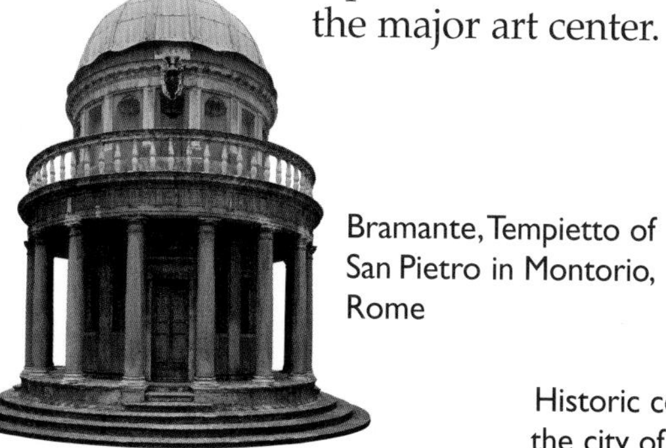

Bramante, Tempietto of San Pietro in Montorio, Rome

Ferrara
Ferrara was one of several splendid Italian courts, along with Mantua, Rimini, Urbino, Milan, and Naples.

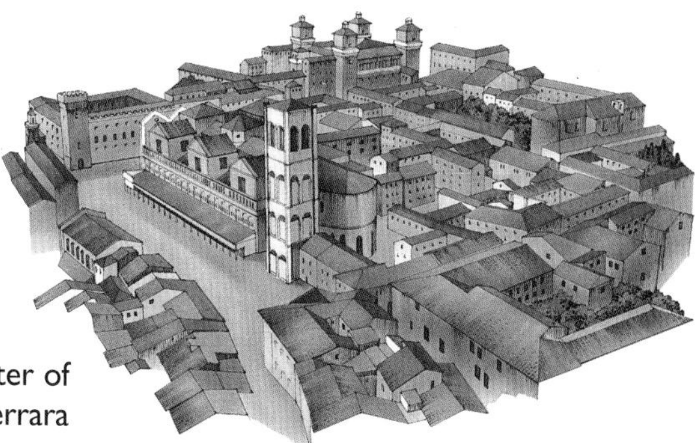

Historic center of the city of Ferrara

Perspective

At the beginning of the 15th century, Florentine artists were trying to represent the real world as faithfully as possible. To do so on flat surfaces such as panels or walls, they had to be able to create a convincing illusion of height and width, and also to convey a sense of the third dimension, depth. The discovery of perspective turned this aspect of art into an exact mathematical science.

A hole in the wall

The first painter to utilize the laws of perspective was Masaccio. In about 1428 he painted a fresco, *The Trinity*, in the church of Santa Maria Novella, Florence: the people who first saw it did not realize it was a painting, believing they were looking through a hole in the wall at a real chapel!

Masaccio (1401–28)

Masaccio died very young. But even so, his works were so powerful and innovative that he is considered the pioneer of Renaissance painting.

The Annunciation

Fra Angelico (c. 1400–55)

Fresco, 7½ x 10½ ft., c. 1438, Museum of San Marco, Florence

Fra Angelico was a monk, and his paintings, mostly in the cells of the monastery of San Marco, express a deep mystical piety. He was among the earliest Florentine masters to absorb the new ideas about painting, which had been discovered by Brunelleschi and applied by Masaccio. *The Annunciation* is an outstanding example of the application of the laws of perspective to the representation of space.

The point of view

The architect and sculptor Brunelleschi discovered the laws of perspective, and Masaccio applied them to the figures and architectural background in *The Trinity*. As a result, looking at the painting produces the same effect as looking at a real chapel, with the figures receding into the distance just as they would in reality. This is shown in the reconstruction.

The colonnade is painted with a visual accuracy made possible by the use of perspective. For example, as shown in the detail of the painting reproduced here, the arches and the capitals at the tops of columns are represented as progressively smaller, just as they would look if they were seen in reality.

Flanders

In northern Europe too, painters were trying to represent figures and backgrounds as realistically as possible. Flemish artists achieved this by meticulously recording the smallest details of everyday life. The greatest of them all, Jan van Eyck, used pigments mixed with oils; though not the inventor of oil painting, he exercised a strong influence in Italy and in the North.

Painting in oil
In the Middle Ages, painters usually prepared their colors by mixing the pigments extracted from plants and minerals with egg; this was known as tempera. Van Eyck began to use oil instead of egg, which made it possible for him to obtain richer colors and more luminous effects.

Portraits
Wealthy Flemings were eager to have their portraits painted. Because it took so long, mannequins with plaster garments were used in their place for part of the time.

The Madonna of Chancellor Nicolas Rolin
Jan van Eyck (c. 1390–1441)
Oil on panel, 26 x 24½ in., c. 1435, Louvre, Paris

The powerful chancellor of Duke Philip the Good kneels before the seated Virgin and child. The sumptuous interior opens on to a balcony from which can be seen a garden and, beyond it, countryside with a river that flows to the horizon. Every part is filled with small but perfect details.

The Birth of Venus
Botticelli (Alessandro Filipepi) (1445–1510)
Tempera on canvas, approx. 5 1/2 x 9 ft., 1483–85, Uffizi, Florence

The goddess Venus is carried to shore on a shell, blown across the water by the breath of the winds; an attendant moves to fling a mantle across her shoulders. This poetic and symbolic painting also illustrates the Florentine preference for strongly drawn outlines.

A Florentine workshop

Benefiting from Masaccio's pioneering efforts, the arts flourished in 15th-century Florence. They were funded by wealthy families who sought to outdo one another as patrons and collectors. At the center of artistic activity were the workshops of leading masters. Here we visit the workshop of Verrocchio in 1469.

Perugino
Having arrived from Umbria, Perugino began by painting on terracotta. Raphael trained in Perugino's workshop.

Andrea Verrocchio
Goldsmith, painter, and sculptor, Verrocchio was also the master of Leonardo, Perugino, and Ghirlandaio.

The furnace
In the workshop there was a bronze foundry which included a stone furnace.

Leonardo Da Vinci

Ghirlandaio

Botticelli

A customer
At first, wealthy Florentines paid for works that were intended for use in churches. Later they began collecting for themselves, while artists tackled secular as well as religious subjects.

The lavabo
Two workers put together a marble water basin ordered for a monastery.

Mona Lisa
Leonardo da Vinci (1452–1519)
Oil on panel, 30 1/4 x 20 3/4 in., 1503, Louvre, Paris

This has become one of the most famous paintings in the world, perhaps because it seems mysterious. Behind Mona Lisa, with her enigmatic smile and calm gaze, is a characteristic Leonardo landscape; its mistiness and fading colors illustrate Leonardo's discoveries about how atmosphere modifies color.

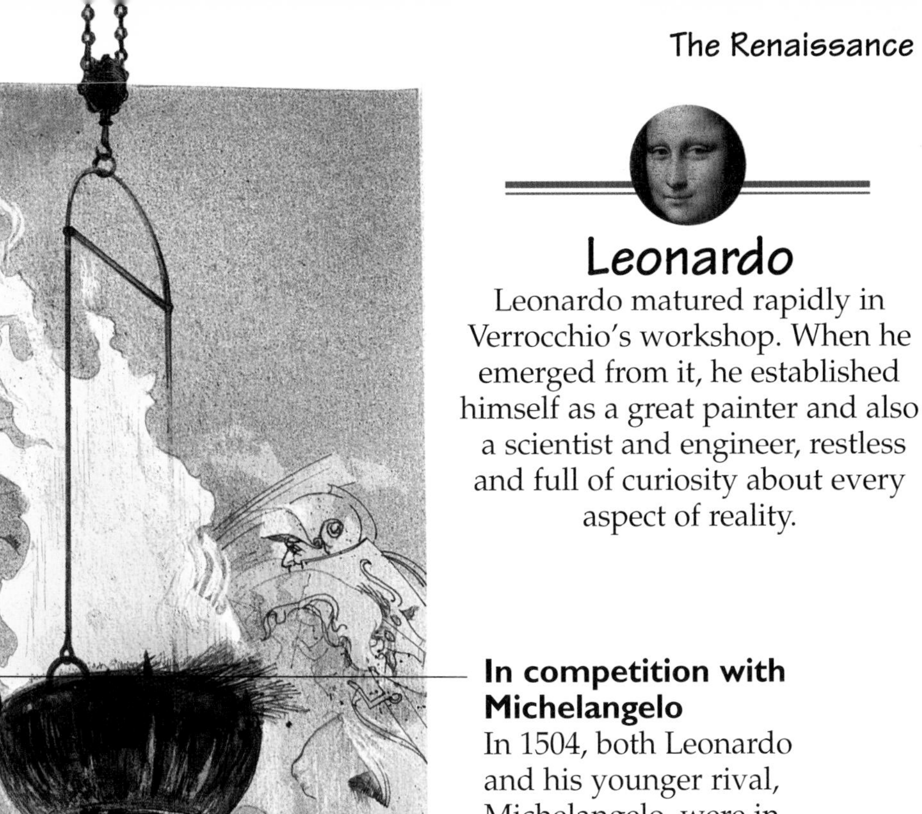

Leonardo

Leonardo matured rapidly in Verrocchio's workshop. When he emerged from it, he established himself as a great painter and also a scientist and engineer, restless and full of curiosity about every aspect of reality.

In competition with Michelangelo
In 1504, both Leonardo and his younger rival, Michelangelo, were in Florence. Each was asked to paint a fresco for the council chamber of the Palazzo Vecchio. Leonardo decided to paint a famous Florentine victory, the battle of Anghiari, using an ancient technique: encaustic.

Encaustic
This technique involved using pigments mixed with wax. Leonardo seems to have made some kind of mistake involving the use of braziers. It caused the colors to run, ruining the picture.

An invention
Always full of ideas, Leonardo devised a platform that could be raised or lowered by turning a large screw.

The Creation of Adam
Michelangelo Buonarroti (1475–1564)
Fresco, 1508–12, Sistine Chapel, the Vatican, Rome

In the center of the vast ceiling Michelangelo placed a scene based on Genesis, the first book of the Bible: it shows the creation of the first man in God's own image. The future, in the form of not-yet-created Eve, looks out from under God's left arm.

On the ceiling
For almost four years, with little help, Michelangelo worked on high scaffolding, painting the ceiling of the Sistine Chapel. Only unimportant tasks were carried out by assistants.

Michelangelo

The great Florentine artist Michelangelo was summoned to Rome by Pope Julius II. Though trained as a sculptor, he painted the ceiling of Julius's private chapel, the Sistine, and in doing so created a titanic masterpiece.

The cartoon
The cartoon was a full-scale preliminary drawing with holes pricked out along the drawn lines. It was laid over the fresh plaster.

The dusting
Charcoal dust was rubbed (pounced) onto the cartoon. Some passed through the holes; then the cartoon was removed, leaving dotted guidelines.

Raphael

The painter Raphael was the third great master (with Leonardo and Michelangelo) of the High Renaissance. Unlike Michelangelo, he was gentle and sociable, taking pleasure in working alongside his most talented pupils.

The arriccio
A young assistant spreads the first rough layer of plaster, the arriccio, over the wall.

Stanza della Segnatura
The Stanza della Segnatura was a room in the Vatican. While Raphael worked in it, Michelangelo was not far away, painting the Sistine Chapel.

The School of Athens

Raphael Sanzio (1483–1520)

Fresco, base $25\frac{1}{4}$ ft., 1509–10, Stanza della Segnatura, the Vatican, Rome

An imaginary gathering of ancient Greek philosophers, with Plato and Aristotle in the center, is framed by an arch. These classical thinkers were vital to the development of Renaissance ideas.

The workshop
The medieval tradition of the craft workshop continued all through the Renaissance. The master left many tasks to assistants, reserving the most skilled operations for himself.

The plaster
The second, damp layer of plaster was covered with the cartoon so that the assistants could use the dusting technique (page 73) to outline the design.

Piercing
A boy pierces holes in the cartoon, making it ready for dusting.

The master
The master controls all aspects of the work from a distance.

The Rialto Bridge
The Rialto Bridge is the oldest and most famous bridge in Venice, carrying a street of shops across the Grand Canal.

A building site
In Venice, building required techniques adapted to the city's unusual circumstances: the area to be built on first had to be carefully fenced off from the canal.

Venice

Venice was originally built on the islands in a lagoon; the waters separating the islands were bridged and became the city's famous canals. In art, while the Florentines favored lines, Venetian painters loved color.

Pile foundations
The foundations of Venetian buildings are huge wooden piles, driven down into the seabed.

Virgin and Child

Giovanni Bellini (c. 1432–1516)

Oil on canvas, $46\frac{1}{2}$ x $33\frac{1}{2}$ in., 1508, Brera Museum, Milan

During his long career, the great Venetian painter Giovanni Bellini mainly produced devotional scenes for the altars of churches. His art combines rich color and intensity of light with great delicacy in rendering facial expressions and a mastery of landscape backgrounds.

The Adoration of the Magi
Albrecht Dürer (1471–1528)
Oil on panel, 39 1/2 x 45 in., 1504, Uffizi, Florence

The scene is an immaculate example of a perspective composition. Dürer deploys the ruined arches to create a sense of space and a stagelike setting for the main figures. The Magi look almost incongruous in their sumptuous clothes.

Printing
Printing from movable type was introduced in Germany in the 15th century, providing the necessary conditions for the development of the modern world.

Germany

At the end of the 15th century, the Renaissance spread to Germany and stimulated an artistic flowering. Great painters such as Grünewald, Cranach, and Dürer produced religious works of great expressive intensity.

Woodcuts
In its early days, printing was an engraver's art: a skilled craftsman used a knife to cut out letters and designs.

Typesetting
Johann Gutenberg made a decisive advance, using movable type that could be rearranged and reused.

The printing press
Equally important was the press on which printing could be mechanically carried out.

The golden age

Renaissance art was essentially realistic – a movement toward accurate representation of the visible world. There were more great Renaissance masters than there is space to mention here. We have not been able to visit the splendid courts of Italy or look at works by, for example, Piero della Francesca, the Venetians Giorgione and Titian, the Flemings van der Weyden and Pieter Bruegel, the Germans Cranach and Grünewald, or the French artist Jean Fouquet. In Italy, around 1520, the High Renaissance created a conviction that art had reached perfection and nothing new could be done. The next generation devoted itself to imitation or scholarship or showiness. The golden age had ended.

The Rise of Europe

From the 16th to the 19th century, Europe grew wealthier and stronger at a rate not seen before. Europeans traveled, conquered native peoples, and settled all over the world, until they completely dominated it. Printing, the compass, oceangoing ships, and firearms played a vital role in these developments, which would eventually lead to the creation of a global economy. Three great events changed the history of humanity: the scientific revolution of the 17th century; the late 18th-century French Revolution, which spread ideas of democracy and nationalism; and the Industrial Revolution, which ushered in an age of unequaled economic and technological advance.

David, *The Death of Marat*

Our journey

For a very long time, European art was based on the principles and techniques established during the Renaissance. From about 1550 to 1850, styles such as Baroque, Rococo, Neoclassicism, and Romanticism followed one another in painting, sculpture, and architecture, but although there were big differences between them, none of them made a fundamental break with the Renaissance tradition. This is not to say that there were no innovative artists. Soon after the end of the Renaissance there was, for example, the painter Caravaggio (pages 82–83). Another towering figure was Bernini (pages 84–85), whose sculpture and architecture reflected the power and splendor of the Church, absolute monarchs, and great aristocratic families. The meticulous everyday quality of Flemish painting was carried into the 17th century by the Dutch painters. The golden age of Holland was represented by Rembrandt (pages 86–87) and Vermeer (pages 88–89). In the 17th and 18th centuries, kings and princes ordered the building of vast palaces that were theatrical and ornate, employing decorative artists such as Tiepolo (pages 90–91). Toward the end of the 18th century, new versions of Classicism appeared, championed by, among others, the sculptor Canova (pages 92–93). As the 18th century turned into the 19th, a new sensibility developed that was expressed with force by the Spanish painter Goya (pages 94–95).

Paris
In 1789, the domination of French society by royals and aristocrats broke down. The French Revolution proclaimed the ideals of liberty, equality, and fraternity and waged war on the great European powers.

Bernini, bust of Louis XIV

Versailles
Built in the mid-17th century for Louis XIV of France, the splendid Palace of Versailles was the center and symbol of his absolute power.

Velázquez, *Las Meninas*

Spain
Spanish power reached its zenith in the late 16th century under King Philip II. But Spain's greatest painter, Velázquez, belonged to the 17th century, when the country was politically in decline.

Great Britain
During the 18th century, England and Scotland united to form Great Britain. The British founded a large colonial empire and underwent an Industrial Revolution that made their country a world power.

Turner, *Calais Pier*

Holland
Independent from the late 16th century, Holland was run by a wealthy merchant elite. It became a leading commercial and maritime power in the 17th century.

Hals, *Banquet of the Officers of the St. George Militia Company*

Germany
Ravaged by the Thirty Years War (1618–48), Germany was impoverished and remained divided into many separate states. In the 18th century the state of Prussia emerged as a leading military power.

Frederick II of Prussia, by an unknown artist

Rome
Threatened by the spread of Protestantism, the popes responded by promoting an art of conscious magnificence and theatricality to emphasize the might and majesty of the Catholic Church.

Borromini, façade of the church of Sant'Agnese, Rome

The Calling of Saint Matthew

Michelangelo Merisi, known as Caravaggio (1571–1610)

Oil on canvas, $10\frac{1}{2}$ x 11 ft., c. 1599, San Luigi dei Francesi, Rome

In a darkened room, five tax collectors count their day's takings. Jesus and Peter (with his back to us) point to Levi, a collector who, under the name Matthew, will become Jesus' disciple and one of the evangelists. The dramatic use of light and shade emphasizes the grouping of the figures and the significance of the moment.

Caravaggio

Caravaggio led a turbulent life and shocked conservatives by introducing many new ideas into painting. He showed biblical figures as ordinary people in humble everyday settings.

The canvas

Caravaggio's canvases were prepared with a ground (preparatory layer) of glue, oil, white lead, and earth colors; then he began the painting with oil colors.

The studio
Above all a master of light and shade, Caravaggio worked in a darkened studio, using carefully arranged curtains to filter the light.

The models
For religious subjects, Caravaggio painted his figures in contemporary dress and everyday surroundings.

Straight onto canvas
Unlike most artists of his time, Caravaggio did not use preliminary drawings. He put an outline onto the canvas and then painted from life, straight onto it.

The Ecstasy of St. Teresa
Gian Lorenzo Bernini (1598–1680)
Marble and bronze, 1647–52, church of Santa Maria della Vittoria, Rome

Bernini and many other Baroque artists aimed to bring together the visual arts of architecture, painting, and sculpture. Here, the vault of heaven painted in the niche, the sculptural group, and the architectural setting create a single, overwhelming spectacle: the rapture of a saint consumed by God's love.

Baroque Rome

In the 17th century, Rome was the capital of Catholic Europe. It was also the center of the new Baroque style, in which buildings, sculptures, and paintings were sweeping, theatrical, and ornate, expressing the power and splendor of the Church.

Bernini
In 1637, Pope Alexander VII ordered Bernini to redesign the layout of St. Peter's Square. This is where, every Easter, Catholics congregate in huge numbers in order to affirm their faith and receive the papal blessing.

Optical illusions
Each wing of the colonnade consists of four rows of columns. Through an optical illusion, from two places in the square there appears to be only a single row.

The colonnade
Bernini's colonnade comprises two majestic curving wings, like the motherly arms of the Church.

Master and pupils
In Rembrandt's studio, the most famous in Holland, master and pupils often worked together around the model.

Properties
Rembrandt had a taste for painting unusual objects, and his studio was full of statues, armor, exotic costumes, and other curiosities.

The Night Watch
Rembrandt van Rjin (1606–69)
Oil on canvas, 12 x 14½ ft., 1642, Rijksmuseum, Amsterdam

In 17th-century Holland, one of the most popular types of painting was the group portrait. Civic bodies and members of guilds and other associations paid to be shown together as banqueters, in consultation, or in heroic poses and costumes. This was how the Civic Guard of Amsterdam chose to be represented. Rembrandt created a brilliantly effective play of light.

Holland

By contrast with the Baroque grandeur of Catholic Europe, Protestant countries generally favored more sober arts. In the 17th century, Holland, though small, enjoyed a thriving economy and cultural life. Dutch painters excelled in portraiture and everyday scenes. The greatest was Rembrandt.

Dutch painters
Unlike medieval and Renaissance artists, Dutch masters often painted pictures before finding buyers for them. This modern practice was possible because a large middle class was eager to purchase pictures. However, it made the artist's position less certain and condemned the unsuccessful to poverty.

Jan Vermeer
Vermeer painted many pictures that are set in the same room, and this has led to the belief that he used a camera obscura. When such a device is used, the image of the room is projected upside down onto the surface of the canvas, allowing the artist to copy the details and light effects.

The camera obscura

Important scientific advances were made in 17th-century Holland, especially in optics and lensmaking. The camera obscura enabled an artist to project an image onto a flat surface; he could then work on this image directly, without having to make laborious calculations to establish the correct proportions and perspective.

The Artist's Studio

Jan Vermeer (1632–75)
Oil on canvas, approx. 47 x 39 in., 1672, Kunsthistorisches Museum, Vienna

Vermeer painted intimate scenes of middle-class domestic life. He paid great attention to the relationships between the figures, the performance of ordinary tasks (such as pouring milk and sewing), the quality of the light, and to creating a sense of space. *The Artist's Studio* shows a painter at work, intent on capturing the appearance of the model, who seems to be posed as a figure symbolizing Glory. It has usually been thought that the man at the easel is Vermeer himself, although so little is known of the painter's life or artistic practices that we cannot be sure. Maps, like the one at the back, were decorative items found in many Dutch homes, thanks to maritime trade and the taste for cartography that seafaring promoted.

A domestic setting
Jan Vermeer and Rembrandt were the greatest masters of 17th-century Dutch painting, although there were many other outstanding figures. Only 35 paintings have been identified that are definitely by Vermeer.

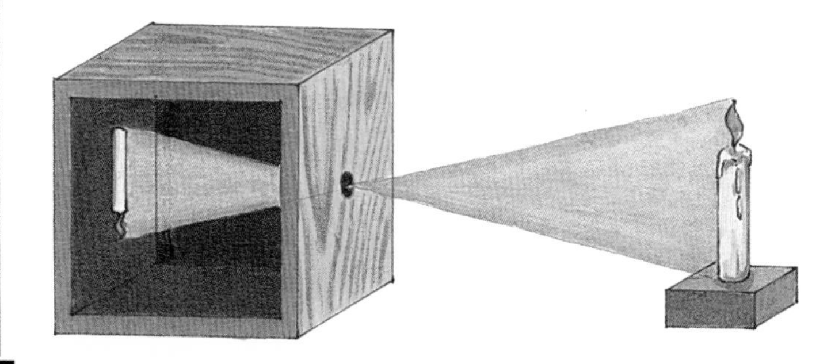

In the throne room
Tiepolo painted a fresco celebrating the glory of the Spanish Bourbon dynasty. He filled it with mythological and historical references.

In Madrid
In 1762 the King of Spain, Charles III, commissioned the Italian painter Tiepolo to decorate the throne room of the royal palace in Madrid with frescoes.

The great decorators

Kings and princes in 18th-century Europe displayed their greatness by building palaces and decorating them sumptuously. Italian artists worked all over Europe, decorating interiors for royal and aristocratic patrons; they were famous for their elegant plasterwork and panoramic frescoes on the walls and ceilings of palaces, mansions, and monasteries.

The Banquet of Antony and Cleopatra
Giambattista Tiepolo (1696–1770)
Fresco, approx. 21 x 10 ft., 1747–50, Palazzo Labia, Venice

Tiepolo framed and organized his paintings of historical subjects as though the events in them took place on a grand stage. Often the picture was painted high on a wall or ceiling and had to be skillfully designed in order to be best viewed from a distance or from below. *The Banquet* painted by Tiepolo was an extravagant display in which ever more lavishly prepared courses were served, culminating in the celebrated moment, shown here, when Cleopatra dissolves a pearl in vinegar simply to show off her wealth.

Paoline Borghese
Antonio Canova (1757–1822)
Marble, approx. 6½ ft. long, 1807, Borghese Gallery, Rome

In 1802 the Italian sculptor Canova was summoned to Paris to portray Napoleon Bonaparte, at that time the First Consul of France. After carrying out this task, Canova continued to be patronized by the Bonaparte family. He represented Napoleon's favorite sister, Pauline, Princess Borghese (above), as Venus Victorious, the goddess of love worshiped by the ancient Greeks and Romans.

Neoclassicism

In the 18th century there was a renewed interest in the ancient world, which became better understood thanks to excavations at Pompeii and Herculaneum, two Roman cities found buried under volcanic ash. Artists aimed to recapture the "calm grandeur and noble simplicity" of classical works.

Using calipers
An assistant uses calipers to check that the measurements of the plaster model, scaled up, correspond with those of the master's small clay model.

Models
After making some sketches, Canova produced a scale model in clay, followed by a model in plaster. Finally he copied the plaster model in marble.

The great sculptor
Antonio Canova was probably the greatest sculptor of the Neoclassical period. His figures were carved with soft lines in pale, smooth marble, and were arranged in simple, harmonious poses.

Plumb lines
A pair of identical frames are suspended over the plaster model and over the marble block from which the work is to be carved. Plumb lines hanging from the frames provide points of reference, to make sure the copy is faithful.

Visitors
Canova lived in Rome until 1779. Many artists and people visiting the city as part of the traditional Grand Tour came to see his studio.

The Family of Charles IV
Francisco Goya (1746–1828)
Oil on canvas, 110¼ x 132¼ in., 1801, Prado, Madrid

Painted when the French Revolution threatened the kings of Europe, this group portrait may have been ordered to assert the authority of Spain's rulers. But Goya shows them just as he sees them: the queen is haughty and vain, the king a worn mediocrity. The poses are solemn and the costumes glittering, but this is clearly a dynasty in decline.

The queen
The queen is being painted by Goya in the royal palace, the Escorial. Hairdressers, dressmakers, and personal attendants try to make her look her best.

The courtier
The queen's favorite, Manuel Godoy, is the country's real ruler but neglects his duties in order to supervise the painter's work.

Francisco Goya

The long life of this great Spanish painter coincided with an era of European upheaval and the invasion of his native land. Though a court painter, he was also a free spirit, depicting the horrors of war and intolerance, and probing the darker areas of the human personality.

The horse
Although the queen is posing on a stool, Goya's painting will show her on horseback, proudly in control of her steed.

European masters

During the 17th, 18th, and 19th centuries, each European country developed its own artistic school. In fact, works of art are commonly classified by century and country of origin (17th-century Spanish, 18th-century French, and so on). We have not been able to name every great master. Among 17th-century figures who should be mentioned are the Spanish painters El Greco and Velázquez, the Flemings Rubens and van Dyke, Holland's Frans Hals, and France's Nicholas Poussin and Georges de la Tour. Important 18th-century artists include Watteau (France) and Hogarth (England). Goya's contemporaries included French artists Géricault and Delacroix, the German Caspar David Friedrich, and a great British Romantic painter, J. M. W. Turner.

Africa and the Pacific

At the end of the 15th century, Europeans began to explore, conquer, and settle lands beyond the seas and oceans. Over the following centuries they came into contact with societies and cultures which they had not known existed. For the first time, their maps showed the Pacific islands and waters of Oceania, and they began to learn about Black Africa, below the Sahara. Alongside advanced and flourishing cultures, they found peoples whose way of life was technologically undeveloped, but whose rich cultures and beliefs were reflected in striking art forms.

Our journey

The Aboriginal peoples of Australia had long been cut off from any contacts with Asia. Their way of life, as nomadic hunter-gatherers, was very primitive, and the art they produced was of a kind quite unfamiliar to Europeans (pages 98–99). Very different again were works by sculptors of the Benin Empire in West Africa (pages 100–1). These works showed that there was a rich culture in the African continent before European colonization began; in fact there were a variety of specialized occupations, flourishing commerce, and sophisticated art forms. For a long time the peoples of Oceania were free from outside interference and able to practice their traditional arts. The population was divided into three main groups: Melanesians, Micronesians, and Polynesians. Polynesian wood-carving was of exceptional quality, and the colossal and mysterious stone sculptures of Easter Island (pages 102–3) provoked strong emotions and controversies that have continued until today. Oceanic and African art, though often described as "primitive art," came to be admired in the West (pages 104–5). Many artists have tried to create similar simple forms and to capture the essence of a subject without putting in large numbers of realistic details. They have also been influenced by the idea that "primitive" societies can show Westerners how to live with nature in a balanced and harmonious way.

Timbuktu, Mali

The empire of Mali
In the 14th century, the capital of Mali, Timbuktu, was a lively cultural center. Its university and library were widely famed.

Head of a queen from Benin

Benin
A powerful empire was created around the mouth of the Niger River. From the 14th century it grew rich on trade with Europeans, in slaves, ivory, and gold. Benin bronzes are world famous.

The Congo Basin
In the 16th and 17th centuries the Luba, Kuba, and Lunda peoples established themselves in what are now the states of Congo and Angola, in a belt of savannah cut off by rainforest to the north and desert to the south.

Mother and child, from the Democratic Republic of the Congo

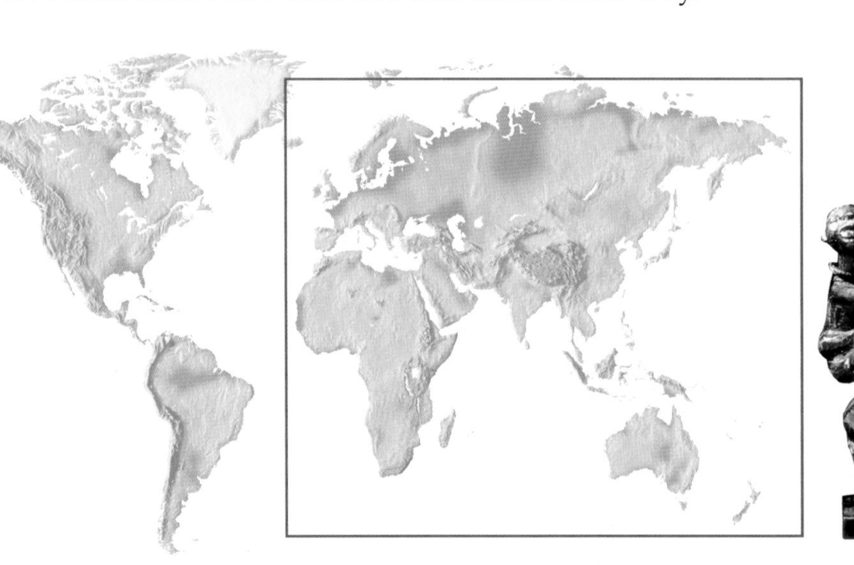

New Guinean mask

New Guinea

New Guinea (Irian Jaya and Papua New Guinea) is the largest island in the Southern Hemisphere, inhabited by many peoples who have widely different cultures and languages. The woodcarving and other arts of this area are of great importance because of their quality and diversity.

Prow of a canoe

Zimbabwe

In southern Africa, the empire of Zimbabwe developed in the 14th and 15th centuries, thanks to its trade in gold with Arab merchants.

Australia

Some 50,000 years ago, falling sea levels created a land link that enabled humans to cross from Asia and settle in Australia.

Oceania

The first inhabitants of the Pacific islands were navigators of extraordinary skill. They sailed in light craft across open water for thousands of miles, using the flight of birds and rudimentary charts to find their way.

Oval enclosure, Zimbabwe

Australian Aborigines

Australia

In the Australian deserts it is possible to find Aboriginal works in the form of hand or body prints or paintings on rock surfaces. These were done as part of religious rituals, but they only lasted for a limited time because of the action of the sun and wind in wearing them away.

Body painting
The Australian Aborigines painted their bodies with designs that had religious and magical meanings.

Making prints
The shape of a hand, or sometimes an entire body, was put onto a rock surface by a simple technique. Artists dissolved pigment with saliva, then sprayed it around the hand or body, which was held against the wall.

Bark painting
Northern Australia (Arnhem Land)
Luigi Pigorini National Prehistoric and Ethnographic Museum, Rome

One of the most vividly expressed Aboriginal art forms is bark painting. Even in a culture with few tools, the materials could be obtained without difficulty, since the bark peeled away easily from the trunks of eucalyptus trees. On this surface the artist painted, among other things, animals such as reptiles, kangaroos, and snakes. The style employed was highly unusual, and has sometimes been described as "X-ray art": the Aborigine painted not only the outside of the creature in question, but also its imagined interior, so that it was provided with a kind of skeleton.

Colors
The number and type of colors used in Aboriginal art stayed the same through the ages: white from chalk, yellowish-red from minerals, and black from a charcoal made from burned and crushed plants.

Head of a queen mother
Bronze, 19 1/2 in. high,
Museum für Völkerkunde, Berlin

We do not know when this head was made, though it is usually placed around the 16th century. Benin craftsmen cast bronze heads of the king and of the queen mother, after their deaths. The heads were to commemorate the individuals concerned, but were also placed on the altars dedicated to them and honored with processions and sacrifices. The queen mother wears an elegant beaded cap and a ringed collar covering her neck. (In some other examples the collar is much higher, covering part of the face.) The portrait (for instance, the composed expression and symmetrical features) is not entirely realistic – probably to distance the queen mother from other humans and convey her divine origin.

Benin

Benin was the capital of a great West African kingdom. In the 15th century European visitors were impressed by its walls, and by its size and highly organized society. Benin craftsmen produced a sophisticated art, using what is usually described as bronze (copper and tin), although it is actually brass, an alloy of copper and zinc.

Altars
The altars of royal ancestors were placed in the courtyard of the royal palace. There was a separate altar for each dead king.

The king
On his throne, the king was surrounded with bronze heads of guards, elephant tusks, wooden staffs, and brass bells used to attract good spirits and drive away evil ones.

Ceremonial processions
Many processions were held during the year, usually in connection with farming tasks. Some were more secret and took place inside the royal palace.

Oceania

Artists in Oceania carved wood and stone to make sculptures or ritual masks. Widespread artistic practices included the decoration of human skulls and the art of tattooing.

The moai
Rapa Nui, renamed Easter Island by European voyagers, lies in the Pacific, 1,100 miles from any other land. It is famous for its moai, colossal stone statues with coral eyes.

Clan rivalry
The figures weigh up to 80 tons and stand between $6^1/_2$ and 33 feet high. They owed their size partly to the rivalry between the island's clans, each trying to outdo the others.

Transportation
Made of stone taken from the volcano of Rano Raraku, the statues were probably transported using trunks of the only species of tree on the island. If so, this was one cause of deforestation and the impoverishment of the soil.

Ancestor god

Ironwood figure, Rurutu, Tubuai Islands, British Museum, London

A'a was an ancestor of the most important clan on Rurutu, one of the Tubuai Islands in the South Pacific. As happened in many cultures, he came to be regarded as a god. The wood carving is covered with tiny figures in relief, representing his offspring, to whom he is giving life. A movable lid in the torso reveals a hollow containing more small figures like those on the outside.

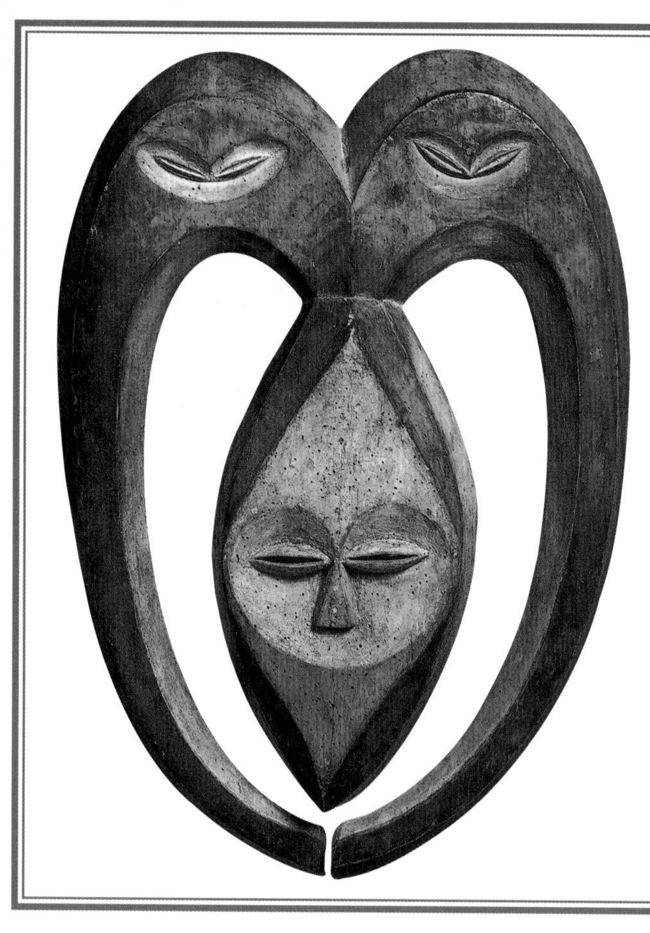

Mask

Wood, 20¾ in. high, Gabon, Kwele

African art did not express individual feelings, but the outlook of the tribe. It was made for use in social activities and group rituals. It was not realistic, but was usually linked with magical and supernatural powers. Themselves magical, masks or figures served to attract benevolent forces and drive away evil ones. The witch doctor's mask showed the power he could put into a look. Warriors had small sculptures representing energy and courage. A figure of a woman and child ensured fertility. And so the themes of motherhood, ancestral presences, and war are found again and again in African art.

The gallery
In the 1930s the dealer Charles Ratton ran a gallery in Paris that displayed a fine selection of African art.

Into the world
Major museums began to ask Ratton to arrange exhibitions of African art for them.

Primitivism

At the beginning of the 19th century, African masks and figures began to be admired by Europeans. Artists were among the first people to study and draw inspiration from such works.

In America
In 1937, Ratton showed 100 objects in a great all-African exhibition in Chicago.

Out of Africa

In the 19th and 20th centuries, European artists became interested in art objects produced by cultures distant from them. Gauguin, Picasso, Matisse, and others found inspiration in African tribal masks or in wood or stone idols from Oceania. Artists still draw inspiration from these arts. It was not the first time that Westerners had turned to the past or to exotic arts; as we have seen, Greek and Roman art were constantly being reinterpreted. But a new element in Western interest in African and Oceanic art was that attention was paid not just to what objects represented but to how they were represented, to the way in which form and meaning were united. Curiosity about other cultures also led to a recognition of the importance of all artistic activity.

Break with Tradition

The Industrial Revolution, and the transformation of the world that followed it, had a profound impact on Western art. From the mid-19th century onward, radically new artistic styles and idioms appeared in Europe. Artists were seen in a new light, as creators who were entitled to determine the content and style of their works. Europe, though still dominating most of the world, began to lose faith in its old certainties. And in the 19th and 20th centuries, Europeans were faced with many new realities: sprawling cities, rapid social change, mass movements and ideologies, scientific discoveries, and the horrors of war and genocide.

Our journey

In mid-19th-century Paris, artists working in new styles met with great hostility when their works were shown in public (pages 108–9). Soon after this, artists began to leave their studios in order to paint in the open air, breaking with a centuries-old tradition of picture-making. Monet and Renoir spent time at a resort on the Seine River and recorded the lively scene on two canvases (pages 110–11). In early 20th-century Europe, the urge to experiment with new forms and to deal with contemporary realities and feelings led to the founding of several avant-garde movements. Among the most important were Futurism, Cubism, and Expressionism (pages 114–15). Two of the many famous 20th-century artists who made a particularly deep impression were Marc Chagall (pages 116–17) and Pablo Picasso (pages 118–19). The scorn with which people greeted other experiments, for example those of the Surrealists (pages 120–21), showed that there was a gulf between the aims and ideas of 20th-century artists and the attitudes of the general public. Architecture in the 20th century (pages 122–23) also involved revolutionary ideas, breaking with the standards that had been introduced by Brunelleschi during the early Renaissance and followed for 500 years. In the meantime, an astonishingly wide variety of styles and techniques were practiced in painting and sculpture as the end of the century approached (page 124).

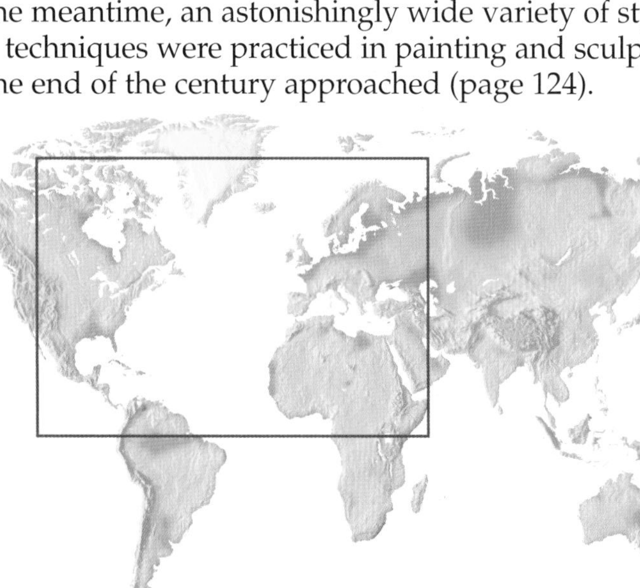

Courbet, *Young Women on the Banks of the Seine*

Paris
During the reign of Emperor Napoleon III, industrialization went ahead rapidly. From the 19th century, Paris was the capital of world art. There, Courbet's realism evolved, followed by Impressionism, Divisionism, Picasso's Cubism, and Surrealism.

New York
After 1945 New York became a vital center of new movements such as Abstract Expressionism and Pop Art. New museums such as the Metropolitan and the Guggenheim made New York a city of great collections.

The Empire State Building, New York

Barbizon
This village close to Fontainebleau gave its name to a school of landscape painters, of whom the best known was Théodore Rousseau.

Rousseau, *Forest of Fontainebleau, Morning*

Kandinsky, first abstract watercolor

Munich
The movement in painting known as the Blaue Reiter (Blue Riders) crystallized in Munich in 1910 around the works of Kandinsky and Marc. The Blaue Reiter journal chronicled art of the time.

Berlin
Movements in art and architecture which developed in Berlin at the beginning of the 20th century influenced the avant-garde in other European cities.

Marc, *Red Deer*

Russia
The 1917 Revolution had important repercussions on the arts. The works of Chagall exalted popular culture. Another Russian artist, Wassily Kandinsky, is regarded as the pioneer of abstract art.

Tatlin, *Model for a Monument to the Third International*

Dresden
In 1905 the painter Kirchner founded Die Brücke (The Bridge), which became the most important German Expressionist group.

Dalí, *Premonition of Civil War*

Zurich
This Swiss city was the birthplace of an irreverent movement in art and literature called Dada. Dada exalted the spontaneous and irrational, mounting violent attacks on established values.

Spain
The Spanish painters Picasso, Gris, Miró, and Dalí are considered to be among the most innovative of 20th-century artists.

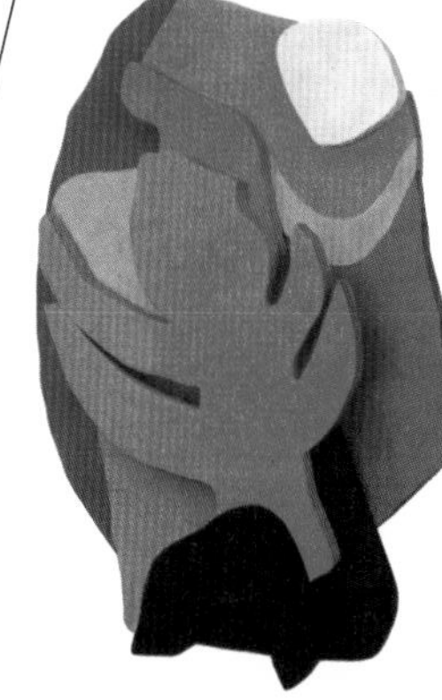
Arp, *Forest*

Kirchner, *Five Women in a Street*

Paris

The Salon was an official exhibition, held every two years, which served as a showcase for French art. The selection jury favored works with traditional historical and mythological ("academic") subjects, and rejected the efforts of less conventional artists.

The site
From 1855 the Salon was held in the Palace of Industry. This iron and glass structure was built by advanced mass-production techniques on the orders of Napoleon III for the 1855 Universal Exhibition.

In 1863
Showing works at the Salon was of decisive importance to an artist's career. In 1863 the jury had to examine thousands of items.

The jury
The jury consisted of academic painters, who rejected the works of less established artists.

Napoleon III
The emperor visited the Salon but also ordered that the rejected works should be exhibited separately in a Salon des Refusés.

Luncheon on the Grass

Edouard Manet (1832–83)

Oil on canvas, approx. 7 x 8¾ ft., 1863,
Musée d'Orsay, Paris

This famous painting was among the works rejected by the Salon jury in 1863 and exhibited in the Salon des Refusés. The picture was condemned at the time as indecent, but it was to become one of the beacons of 19th-century art. Its success lies in Manet's choice of subject, showing people of his own time in a natural setting, and in his painting technique, which gave very different effects from the slick procedures of academic art.

La Grenouillère
Claude Monet (1840–1926)
Oil on canvas, 29 1/2 x 39 1/4 in., 1869, Metropolitan Museum, New York

Monet's great interest was the effects of light; the reflections on the moving water can be seen as the main subject here.

La Grenouillère
Pierre-Auguste Renoir (1841–1919)
Oil on canvas, 26 x 32 in., 1869, Statens Konstmuseum, Stockholm

In contrast with Monet, Renoir showed more interest in the foliage and the costumes of the people. Both painters used rapid brushwork.

Painting in the open air

Painting in the open air was a new practice introduced by the Impressionists. Because the light changed rapidly, there was no time for any preliminary drawing; the painting was done directly onto the canvas.

Summer Sundays
Working among white sails and the rustling of petticoats, the painters sought to put on canvas an immediate impression of what they were looking at.

La grenouillère
The "frog pond" (grenouillère) on the River Seine was a popular spot with Parisians for Sunday outings. It became one of the subjects favored by the Impressionist painters Monet and Renoir, who worked together there in 1869.

LOCATION CANOTS

The subject
Like other Impressionist painters, Monet and Renoir showed a great interest in the everyday life and leisure of city-dwellers.

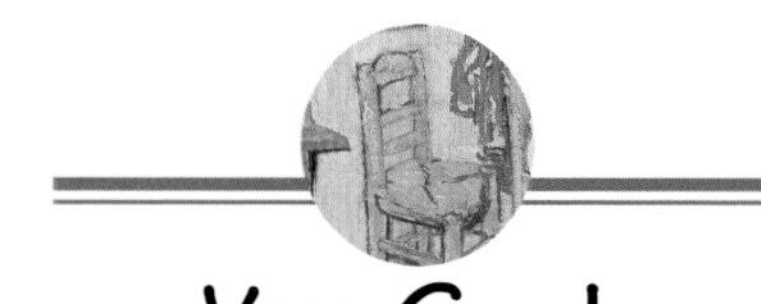

Van Gogh

Restless and eccentric, the Dutch painter Van Gogh made many contributions to late 19th-century art. Above all, he introduced into painting the expression of personal emotion. In moments of serenity he painted with warm colors; in misery, he used cold and sad hues.

Vincent's Bedroom
Vincent van Gogh (1853–90)
Oil on canvas, 22½ x 29 in., 1889, Musée d'Orsay, Paris

During his stay at Arles in the south of France, where he lived in 1888–89, Van Gogh painted everyday things like his own bedroom. Here he employed color in a highly personal way to express his happiness, skillfully balancing the three primary colors and their complementaries: red and green, yellow and violet, blue and orange. White and black are used together in the mirror on the wall.

Box of colors
Van Gogh was able to work rapidly, thanks to oil colors in metal tubes, manufactured from 1846 onward.

The easel
In order to paint *Starry Night over the Rhône*, Van Gogh used an easel that he set up again every time the wind blew it over.

By candlelight
As a mature artist, Van Gogh painted with rapid brushstrokes to capture the appearance of his subject at a given moment and his response to it. To paint at night, he adopted the strange but logical solution of fixing lighted candles onto his straw hat.

The Street
George Grosz (1893–1959)
Oil on cardboard, approx. $12^{3/4}$ x 10 ft., 1915, Staatsgalerie, Stuttgart

A moon in a blood-red sky illuminates disreputable scenes taking place among houses that seem about to collapse. From the start of the First World War (1914–18) German artists turned their attention from the individual to commenting on the ills of society.

The avant-garde

Artists whose ideas are not yet accepted by the public are known as the avant-garde (advanced guard). From the early 20th century, several new movements – Expressionism, Cubism, Futurism – appeared in Europe. Later, even more anti-traditional tendencies, such as abstract art, appeared.

Human misfortune
In Berlin, images of the material and moral damage done by the World War were everywhere: profiteers, prostitutes, fat army contractors, and war-wounded and disabled men.

Berlin
In the early 20th century the German capital, Berlin, provided a notable example of a European metropolis filled with contradictions such as extremes of wealth and poverty. These were soon accentuated by evidence of the horrors of war.

Expressionism
The Expressionist movement appeared at about the same time in several German cities such as Dresden, Munich, and Berlin. While Impressionism dealt in happy, delightfully colored scenes, Expressionism was an art of inner brooding and discontent with the state of the world.

The Russian Revolution
In the period of enthusiasm that followed the Russian Revolution of 1917, art was entrusted with great tasks as part of a hoped-for general awakening.

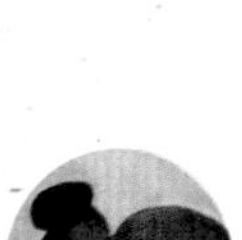

Chagall

Russian Jew and citizen of the world, Marc Chagall lived through most of the 20th century. As a painter he drew inspiration from his origins in Vitebsk and from his experience of family love. He understood both traditional values and new ideas.

Culture for the people
One of the prime objectives of the Revolution was to bring culture to the people. Circulating libraries were created: the books were carried around in wagons.

Vitebsk
In 1919 an academy of popular art and culture was set up in Vitebsk, and the Russian leader Lenin appointed Chagall as its director. The artist organized a festival to celebrate the anniversary of the Revolution.

Artists
Artists worked alongside theater troupes, designing sets and costumes for lively shows explaining the Revolution.

Over Vitebsk
Marc Chagall (1887–1985)
Oil on canvas, 26 x 36 in., 1915–20, MOMA, New York

Here are the houses, fences, and cathedral of Vitebsk. Floating above the snow-covered roofs and street is an aged Jew with his cane and a bundle over his shoulder. As in the long tradition of flying figures in religious art, the atmosphere is one of poetry and miracle, but transferred to an everyday scene.

Paris
Picasso lived in the French capital, Paris, for much of his life. In the summer of 1944, when the city was liberated from the German occupiers, the artist was fêted as a symbol of resistance to fascism.

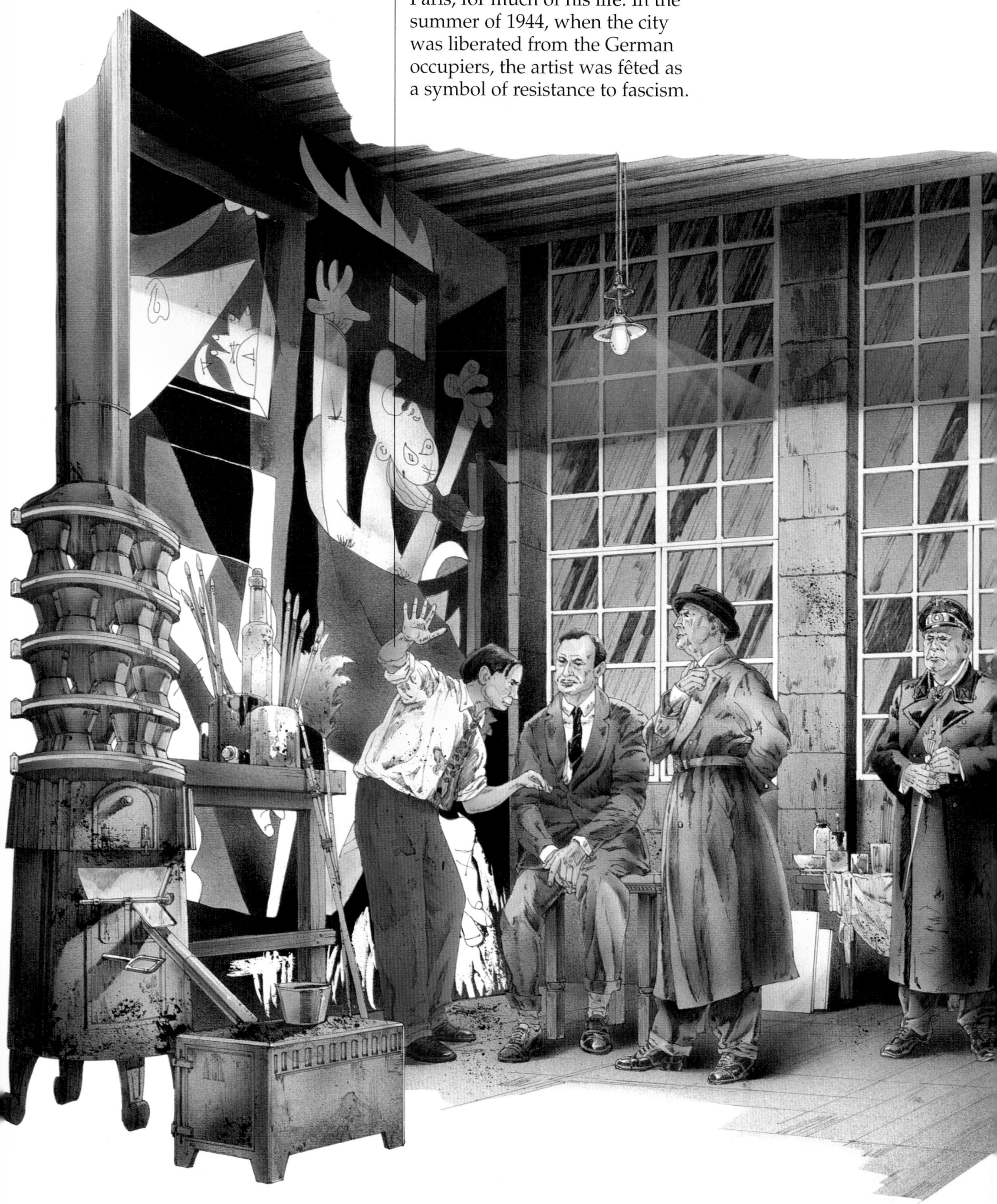

Guernica
Pablo Picasso (1881–1973)
Oil on canvas, 11 1/2 x 25 1/2 ft., 1937, Queen Sofia Art Center, Madrid

During the Spanish Civil War, Nazi German aircraft flew missions on the side of the Spanish fascists. On April 26, 1937, they bombed the Basque city of Guernica, causing widespread death and destruction. Picasso was thinking about painting a picture to show in the Spanish pavilion at the Paris Exhibition. When he heard of the bombing, he set to work on *Guernica*, completing it in just a month. It expresses the ferocity of the assault on Spain. The bull, the horse, and the distorted figures represent the sufferings of the Spanish people, while the black, white, and gray create an appropriately grim atmosphere.

The Nazi occupation of Paris
In 1943, Abetz, the German ambassador to France, is said to have visited Picasso's studio in the Rue des Grands-Augustins. Seeing a reproduction of *Guernica*, he asked "Did you do this?" "No, you did!" replied the artist.

Picasso

Pablo Picasso is the 20th century's most famous artist: painter, sculptor, potter, printmaker, theater designer, and campaigner for peace. He was one of the originators of the revolutionary Cubist movement, but moved restlessly from style to style, and for that reason his work is uniquely representative of the course of 20th-century art.

The exhibition
On January 7, 1938, an International Exhibition of Surrealism opened at the Galerie des Beaux Arts in Paris. It attracted a curious and bemused public.

The Robing of the Bride
Max Ernst (1891–1976)
Oil on canvas, 51 x 38 in., 1940, Peggy Guggenheim Collection, Venice

After a childhood spent in his native Germany, Max Ernst developed a passion for the world of the imagination and unbridled fantasy, extending even to magic and occultism. His paintings are expressions of these preoccupations, recording his hallucinatory visions and the strange female and bird forms that always obsessed him. In this picture, a fierce, armed bird stands guard over the "bride." The top of the feathered mantle worn by the bride takes the form of a bird of prey.

Surrealist Street
Twenty mannequins in strange and extravagant poses were displayed down one side of a wall.

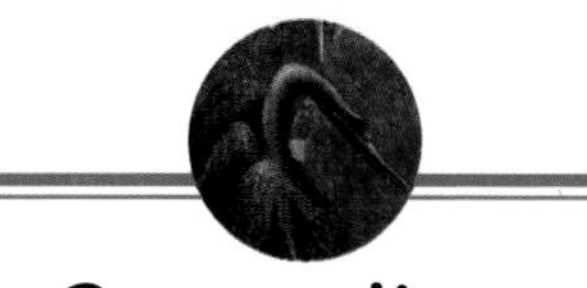

Surrealism

As well as the ordinary, daylight world of understandable actions and emotions, there is the world of dreams and the unconscious. From the 1920s on, a group of artists, who called themselves Surrealists, sought to represent this other world and to free the imagination from reason and common sense.

The water taxi
Salvador Dalí placed a taxi at the entrance of the exhibition; in it were two mannequins that were continually bombarded with jets of water.

Villa Savoye
Charles-Edouard Jeanneret, known as Le Corbusier (1887–1965)
1927, Poissy, near Paris

In the 20th century, buildings were less obviously designed to celebrate the wealth and power of rulers, owners, and municipalities, and most attention was paid to function (that is, practicality). One example is this villa, a boxlike construction in reinforced concrete, designed by the Swiss architect Le Corbusier. Its main living area is surrounded by long glass windows which flood it with light and create panoramic views for those inside. The villa is raised on pillars, called pilotis, and the area beneath provides garage space and an entrance foyer leading by a spiral staircase to the living quarters.

The spiral
In 1957–59 Wright created a spiral structure for the museum. Visitors take the elevator straight to the top, then descend on foot, viewing the collection down a continuous ramp. Their visit ends, conveniently, at the exit.

Architecture

Compared with modern painting, a specifically modern type of architecture was slow to develop. But when it did, it brought profound changes to building traditions. The changes were not directly concerned with style and decoration; rather, the modernists were preoccupied above all with the purpose to be served by the structures they were commissioned to design.

The Guggenheim Museum
A great art collector, Solomon Guggenheim, commissioned the famous American architect Frank Lloyd Wright (1867–1959) to construct a building for the most celebrated museum of modern art in the world, the Guggenheim Museum in New York.

The elevator
The elevator carries members of the public to the top floor, where they begin their visit.

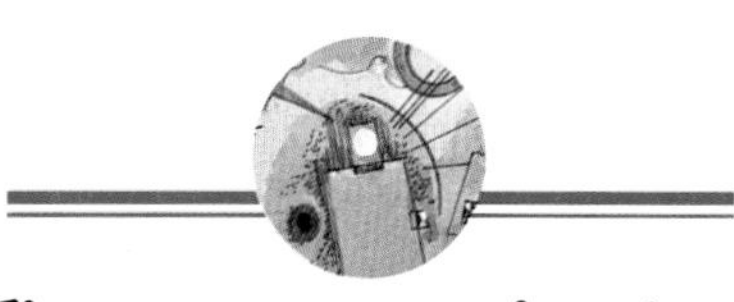

The art revolution

Knowledge of art, and its "consumption" in terms of buying, exhibition visiting, commercial spin-offs, and similar phenomena, have increased enormously in recent years, thanks to affluence and social change.

20th-century styles
In the second half of the 20th century, the art scene has witnessed the birth of many styles and movements, including Art Informel, Pop Art, Superrealism, Arte Povera, and Transavantgarde.

Posters
The works of the most popular or "cult" artists, from Leonardo to Warhol, have become familiar through reproductions on posters. Used to advertise exhibitions, these are bought and treasured as works of art in their own right.

Great exhibitions
Over the last few decades, museums of contemporary art have sprung up in many cities. Besides holding permanent collections, big-city museums host temporary or traveling shows of all kinds.

Reproductions
Magazines, books, postcards, catalogs, videotapes, CD-ROMs: a huge cultural industry, based on advanced reproduction techniques, has made the history of art widely accessible.

The works
Until fairly recently, most works of art could only be studied from black-and-white illustrations or by making long journeys to galleries. Color reproductions and videos now cover many subjects, making research easier and more accurate.

Index